Being in
Balance

Also by

Dr. Wayne W. Dyer

BOOKS
Everyday Wisdom
Getting in the Gap (book-with-CD)
Incredible You! (children's book)
Inspiration
Manifest Your Destiny
No More Holiday Blues
The Power of Intention
A Promise Is a Promise
Pulling Your Own Strings
Real Magic
The Sky's the Limit
Staying on the Path
10 Secrets for Success and Inner Peace
There Is a Spiritual Solution to Every Problem
What Do You Really Want for Your Children?
Wisdom of the Ages
You'll See It When You Believe It
Your Erroneous Zones
Your Sacred Self

All of the above are available at your local
book shop, or may be ordered by visiting:
Hay House UK: **www.hayhouse.co.uk**
Hay House USA: **www.hayhouse.com®**
Hay House Australia: **www.hayhouse.com.au**
Hay House South Africa: **orders@psdprom.co.za**
Hay House India: **www.hayhouseindia.co.in**

Being in Balance

9 Principles for Creating Habits to Match Your Desires

Dr. Wayne W. Dyer

HAY HOUSE

Australia • Canada • Hong Kong
South Africa • United Kingdom • United States

First published and distributed in the United Kingdom by:
Hay House UK Ltd, 292B Kensal Rd, London W10 5BE.
Tel.: (44) 20 8962 1230; Fax: (44) 20 8962 1239. www.hayhouse.co.uk

Published and distributed in the United States of America by:
Hay House, Inc., PO Box 5100, Carlsbad, CA 92018-5100.
Tel.: (1) 760 431 7695 or (800) 654 5126; Fax: (1) 760 431 6948 or (800) 650 5115.
www.hayhouse.com

Published and distributed in Australia by:
Hay House Australia Ltd, 18/36 Ralph St, Alexandria NSW 2015.
Tel.: (61) 2 9669 4299; Fax: (61) 2 9669 4144. www.hayhouse.com.au

Published and distributed in the Republic of South Africa by:
Hay House SA (Pty), Ltd, PO Box 990, Witkoppen 2068.
Tel./Fax: (27) 11 706 6612. orders@psdprom.co.za

Distributed in Canada by:
Raincoast, 9050 Shaughnessy St, Vancouver, BC V6P 6E5.
Tel.: (1) 604 323 7100; Fax: (1) 604 323 2600

The author of this book does not dispense medical advice or prescribe the use of any
technique as a form of treatment for physical or medical problems without the advice of a
physician, either directly or indirectly. The intent of the author is only to offer information
of a general nature to help you in your quest for emotional and spiritual wellbeing. In the
event you use any of the information in this book for yourself, which is your constitutional
right, the author and the publisher assume no responsibility for your actions.

A catalogue record for this book is available from the British Library.

Wayne Dyer's editor: Joanna Pyle   Editorial supervision: Jill Kramer
Cover Design: Leanne Siu   Interior Design: e-Digital Design

ISBN 13: 978-1-4019-1068-6
ISBN 10: 1-4019-1068-8

09 08 07 06   5 4 3 2 1
1st printing, October 2006

Printed in Europe by Imago.

For Elizabeth Crow.
10,000 thank yous for your
magical, loving presence.
It is evident on every page of this book.

For my brother David.
We balanced each other
through all the lean years.
I love you.

Contents

"Want is a growing giant whom the coat of Have was never large enough to cover . . ."

— Ralph Waldo Emerson

Introduction

The concept of balance defines our Universe. The cosmos, our planet, the seasons, water, wind, fire and earth are all in perfect balance. We humans are the only exception.

This book is my attempt to help you restore this natural equilibrium in all aspects of your life. Getting in balance is not so much about adopting new strategies to change your behaviours, as it is about realigning yourself in all of your thoughts so as to create a balance between what you desire and how you conduct your life on a daily basis.

When my editor completed her final reading of this book, she scribbled these words to me on a cover sheet: "Wayne, Being in Balance is great! No one can read this and not come away revitalized. I feel as if I'm back in balance myself." I trust that you will feel the same sense of joyful awakening to the perfect balance of our Universe as you read and adopt these nine principles. It is precisely what I had in mind as I allowed these ideas to flow through me and materialize within these pages.

I love this book. I love the way it feels in my hands, and I love the message it has for you. May you use these principles every day to restore yourself to that perfectly balanced place from which you originated.

— In love and glorious light,
Wayne W. Dyer, Maui, Hawaii

> "True imagination
> is not fanciful day-
> dreaming, it is fire
> from heaven."
> — Ernest Holmes

Chapter One

*An Infinity of Forests
Lies Dormant Within the
Dreams of One Acorn*

*(Balancing Your
Dreams with
Your Habits)*

> "The greatest achievement was
> at first and for a time a dream. The oak
> sleeps in the acorn; the bird sleeps in
> the egg; and in the highest vision of the
> soul, a waking angel stirs. Dreams are
> the seedlings of realities..."
> — James Allen

Chapter One

One of the huge imbalances in life is the disparity between your daily existence, with its routines and habits, and the dream you have deep within yourself of some extraordinarily satisfying way of living. In the quote that opens this chapter, James Allen poetically explains that the dream is the magical realm out of which newly created life emerges. Buried within you is an unlimited capacity for creation, what Allen calls *a waking angel* that's anxious to plant seedlings to fulfil your dreams and your destiny. I simply couldn't resist adding the Ernest Holmes quote describing this dynamic imagination as "fire from heaven".

They're both appropriate invitations and reminders that you need to tend to that burning fire, the dream within you, if living a balanced life is important.

How This Imbalance Shows Up in Your Life

This absence of balance between dreams and habits may be very subtle. It doesn't necessarily reveal itself in the obvious symptoms of heartburn, depression, illness or anxiety—it's more often something that feels like an unwelcome companion by your side, which continually whispers to you that you're ignoring something. There's some often-unidentifiable task or experience that you sense is part of your beingness. It may seem intangible, but you can feel the longing to be what you're intended to be. You sense that there's a higher agenda; your *way of life* and your *reason for life* are out of balance. Until you pay attention, this subtle visitor will continue to prod you to regain your equilibrium.

Think of a balance scale with one side weighted down and the other side up, like a teeter-totter with an obese child on one end and a skinny kid on the other. In this case, the heavy end that tips the scale out of balance is the over-weight kid representing your everyday behaviours: the work you do, the place where you reside, the people with whom you interact, your geographic location, the books you read, the movies you see, and the conversations that fill up your life. It's not that any of these things are bad in and of themselves. The imbalance exists because they're unhealthy for *your* particular life—they simply don't mesh with what you've imagined yourself to be. When it's unhealthy, it's wrong, and on some level you feel that. When you live your life *going through the motions*, it may seem to be convenient, but the weight of your dissatisfaction creates a huge imbalance in the only life you have now.

You're perplexed by the ever-present gnawing feeling of dissatisfaction that you can't seem to shake, that pit-of-the-stomach sensation of emptiness. It shows up when you're sound asleep and your dreams are filled with reminders of what you'd love to be, but you wake and return to pursuing your safe routine. Your dreams are also demanding your attention in waking life when you're petulant and argumentative with others, because in actuality you're so frustrated with yourself that you try to relieve the pressure by venting anger outward. Imbalance masquerades as a sense of frustration with your current lifestyle. If you allow yourself to think about this "fire from heaven", you proceed to rationalize your status quo with explanations and mental meanderings that you know in your heart are excuses because you don't think you have the tools to get in balance.

You may get to a point where you become increasingly hard on yourself and begin seeking medication and other treatment for feelings of inadequacy—and for what's called *depression*.

You'll surely witness yourself feeling more and
more angry and moody, with more frequent
occurrences of minor afflictions such as colds,
headaches and insomnia. As time goes on in this
state of imbalance, there's less enthusiasm for
what has become the drudgery of life. Work is
now even more routine, with even less purpose
and drive. These blahs begin appearing in your
behaviour toward your family and those you
love. You're easily agitated, picking on others for
no apparent reason. If you're able to be honest
with yourself, you recognize that your irritability
stems from being out of balance with the bigger
dream you've always had, but
which is now apparently
slipping away.

When these subtle symptoms surface, it's crucial to explore the kind of energy you're giving to the scale to create balance—or in this case, imbalance. The heavy angst is weighing down your reason for being—but you are the only one who can rebalance this scale of your life. Here are some tools to help you return to a balanced life, beginning with recognizing the ways in which you may be sabotaging yourself.

Mental Energy That Makes the Manifestation of Your Dreams Impossible

Your desire to be and live from greatness is an aspect of your spiritual energy. In order to create balance in this area of your life, you have to use the energy of your thoughts to harmonize with what you desire. Your mental energy attracts what you think about. Thoughts that pay homage to frustration will attract frustration. When you say or think anything resembling *There's nothing I can do; my life has spun out of control, and I'm trapped*, that's what you'll attract—that is, resistance to your highest desires! Every thought of frustration is like purchasing a ticket for more frustration. Every thought that agrees that you're stuck is asking the Universe to send you even *more* of that glue to *keep* you stuck.

The single most important tool to being in balance is knowing that *you and you alone are responsible for the imbalance between what you dream your life is meant to be, and the daily habits that drain life from that dream.* You can create a new alignment with your mental energy and instruct the Universe to send opportunities to correct this imbalance. When you do so, you discover that while the world of reality has its limits, the world of your imagination is without boundaries. Out of this boundless imagination comes the seedling of a reality that's been crying out to be restored to a balanced environment.

Restoring the Balance

The objective of this principle is to create a balance between dreams and habits. The least complicated way to begin is to recognize the signs of habitual ways of being, and then learn to shift your thinking to being in balance with your dreams. So what are your dreams? What is it that lives within you that's never gone away? What inner night-light continues to glow, even if it's only a glimmer, in your thoughts and dreams? Whatever it is, however absurd it may seem to others, if you want to restore the balance between your dreams and your habits, you need to make a shift in the energy that you're contributing to your dreams. If you're out of balance, it's primarily because you've energetically allowed your habits to define your life. Those habits, and the consequences thereof, are the result of the energy you've given them.

In the early stages of the rebalancing process, concentrate on this awareness: *You get what you think about, whether you want it or not.* Commit to thinking about what you want, rather than how impossible or difficult that dream may seem. Give your personal dreams a place to hang out on the balance scale so that you can see them in your imagination and they can soak up the energy they deserve. Thoughts are mental energy; they're the currency that you have to attract what you desire. You must learn to stop spending that currency on thoughts you don't want, even though you may feel compelled to continue your habitual behaviour. Your body might continue, for a while, to stay where it's been trained to be, but meanwhile, thoughts are being aligned with your dreams. The esteemed 19th-century writer Louisa May Alcott phrases this idea in an encouraging and inspiring manner:

Far away in the sunshine are
my highest inspirations.
I may not reach them,
but I can look up and see the beauty,
believe in them and try to
follow where they lead...

Choosing to restore a semblance of balance between your dreams and your habits seems possible with Ms. Alcott's phrases in mind: "look up and see," and "believe in them". The words bring to life an energetic alignment. Rather than putting your thoughts on what is, or what you've habitually thought for a lifetime, you shift to looking up and seeing, and firmly believing in what you see. When you begin to think in this manner, the Universe conspires to work with you, and sends you precisely what you're thinking and believing. It doesn't always happen instantaneously, but once the realignment is initiated in your thoughts, you've begun being in balance.

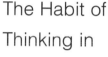

The Habit of Thinking in Alignment with Your Dreams

Oscar Wilde once observed that "We are all in the gutter, but some of us are looking at the stars." This is a perfect example of what it means to align your vision and thoughts so that they're balanced with what you sense you're here to be. A thought such as *It is my intention to create a place to help underprivileged children* is in reality

a message to the Universe. If you feel strongly
that you came here for a particular purpose, then
you should cultivate energy to match this dream.
It doesn't matter what the circumstances of your life
are. Your current financial status is unimportant
when it comes to your pursuit of this purpose. The
presence of a gaggle of naysayers shouldn't sway
you or make you doubt your attraction to your calling. What you're doing as you get your life balanced
with your dream is beginning to co-create your life.

Co-creation is cooperatively using the
energy from the invisible field of Spirit. It is perfectly balancing your in-the-world calling with the pure
energy of creation. You emulate this creation field
by being as much like it as possible. This involves
your willingness to contemplate yourself as a being

of balance attracting the conditions you desire to produce. *It is in the contemplation of this power that you actually acquire this power.* Reread that statement until it sticks with you like superglue. You cannot manifest a place for helping underprivileged children by contemplating the impossibility of that happening. Even if you're in the gutter, you have the option of looking at the stars. This means thinking star thoughts and rejecting the weight of those that attract the gutter. Your balance point is a certainty that you affirm with thoughts along the lines of *I know it, I desire it, it's on its way, nothing can stop it, and there's nothing for me to be upset about.*

This alignment will completely turn your world around. The Universe is based on a Law of Attraction. You'll begin seeing the Universe conspiring with you to attract the right people, the right finances, and the seemingly synchronistic events to turn your dreams into reality, here and now. When you're balanced with thoughts of deserving this cooperation from the world of Spirit, you actively engage in bringing it about. You're enjoying the lightness of being in balance with the creative energy of life. It's no longer possible to sit around complaining or feeling frustrated. You are energized! Why? Because you're balanced with the Source of all creation. And just like it, you access creativity by attracting all that you need with your thoughts. It just doesn't work if you're in a state of imbalance, complaining, living in fear or expecting the worst.

The same logic of realignment for balancing your dream energy with your daily habits applies to anything you're capable of imagining: writing and producing your own music album, training horses, adopting a child from an impoverished land, owning your own home in the country, landing the job that's always eluded you, making the kind of money that will free you from debt, running a marathon... You name it, and if you can dream it, you can achieve it. But only if you align your inner creative energy—your thoughts—so that they match up perfectly with your desires. Thoughts that reinforce current habits that are incongruous with your desire must be replaced with aligned energy.

No one has said it better than Jesus of Nazareth: "Believe that you shall receive and you shall receive." What's the point of living a life disputing such in-balance wisdom?

Chapter Two

*There's More to Life
Than Making It Go Faster*

*(Balancing Your Desire to Enjoy
Life with Your Need to Achieve)*

Chapter Two

The key to balancing your desire to be at peace with your need to achieve, perform, and earn a living is in recognizing that there's no such thing as stress; there are only people thinking stressful thoughts. It's really as simple as that. When you change the way you process the world, the world you're processing changes.

Stress is an inside job. You can't fill a container with it because tension isn't a physical item or object. There isn't some *thing* that you can point to and say, *There it is, that's stress!* It simply doesn't exist in that form. Yet 112 million people in America take medication for stress-related symptoms, which include fatigue, heart palpitations, indigestion, diarrhea, constipation, nervousness, excessive eating, rashes, nail biting, loss of appetite, insomnia, anxiety, irritability, panic, moodiness, memory lapses, the inability to concentrate, ulcers, obsessive-compulsive behaviour, feeling upset... and on and on goes an almost inexhaustible list. And they're all caused by something that doesn't exist in the physical world.

Being out of balance on this stress measure results in being one of the millions of people requiring medication to manage the symptoms listed above. It means that you often feel exasperated because you never really enjoy the life you work so hard to achieve. You may frequently feel as if you're spending your life running on an endless treadmill. All of the pressure of working and striving may have many worldly rewards, yet at the same time there's a feeling of going absolutely nowhere.

If this sounds familiar, it's a signal to begin reconsidering ways of processing thoughts about your life and work, and start pursuing freedom from the symptoms of stress by becoming more balanced. Getting into balance isn't necessarily about changing your behaviour. Certainly you can pursue stress-reducing activities such as meditation, exercise, walks along a beach, or whatever works for you. But if you continue to align yourself with achieving more, defeating the other guy, winning at all costs, and going faster because you believe that's how to keep up, then you're guaranteed to attract the vibrational equivalent of this thinking into your life—even if you do yoga and stand on your head chanting mantras every day!

Stress Reduction Is about Realignment

You become what you think about all day long. You also become how you *think* all day long. To measure the weight of your thoughts, you need to think in terms of vibration and energy. Let's suppose that you have a high-frequency desire to be a person who has no symptoms of stress. Let's assign this thought a 10 on a scale of 1 to 10, with the lowest-energy thought of 1 representing a nervous breakdown, and a 10 representing enlightened, peaceful mastery.

Next, you need to note the thoughts you have that support your desire for a peaceful, stress-free life. Thoughts such as *I'm overwhelmed, I never have enough time, I have so many people wanting things from me that I don't even have time to think, I have so much more on my plate than I can handle, and I feel pressured by my need to make money to pay my bills* aren't balanced and peaceful. These thoughts are resistant energy, which counters the desire for a peaceful, stress-free existence. In other words, they're non-aligned and out of balance. Your desire may be a 10, but your mental energy in this situation is in a much lower range, perhaps a 2 or 3.

Simply changing your behaviour isn't going to get you back into balance. You're still attracting symptoms of stress when you say no to people and their demands, but vibrate to a frequency that's thinking, *I really should be doing what they ask of me,* or *Maybe I can squeeze in their requests later.* You may have pulled back from an overly full and frenzied schedule, yet you continue to radiate thoughts of fear and scarcity that will activate the Law of Attraction to bring you fear and scarcity.

If stress thoughts are tipping the scale, that's what the Law of Attraction brings. Remember: *You become what you think about!* If you're thinking scarcity or anger or fear, guess what? That's what the Law of Attraction attracts! Even with a well-balanced schedule that allows for more free time, and even with plenty of stress-reducing activities on your pared-down personal calendar, if you fail to align your thoughts with the success you're capable of attracting, the weight of the dominant thoughts will tip the scale away from a balanced life. How you live your daily life will remain out of balance, and you'll have failed to assimilate the essence of Gandhi's advice that there is more to life than "increasing its speed".

What you most need to learn is how to create a match between what it is that you desire in your life, and what thoughts, or vibrational energy, you're choosing to attract those desires.

Realigning Your Point of Attraction: The Art of Becoming

Here's one of my favorite quotes from my teacher in India, Nisargadatta Maharaj:

There is nothing to do. Just be.
Do nothing. Be.
No climbing mountains and sitting in caves.
I do not even say "be yourself"
since you do not know yourself.
Just be.

This idea may contradict everything you've been taught and how you've lived so far, but let it sink in anyway. If your lifetime inventory of ideas and rules has contributed to your being one of those 112 million who use medication to handle nonexistent stress, you can certainly afford to entertain this thought. As you begin practising the principles to realign with a vibration that matches your desire for a tranquil, peaceful life, you'll become more conscious of your thoughts. These thoughts of yours literally determine who you are. And the fact that you're reading these words suggests that you're interested in becoming more conscious of your thoughts.

Being and *becoming* are used synonymously here. In order to restore a sense of balance between your desire for tranquility and your desire to meet the requirements of your life, you must practise *becoming*, and *being* the vibration that you desire.

— **Being peace:** Peace isn't something that you ultimately receive when you slow down the pace of your life. Peace is what you're capable of being and bringing to every encounter and event in the waking moments of your life. Most of us are waging a nonstop internal mental skirmish with everyone we encounter. Being peaceful is an inner attitude that you can enjoy when you've learned to silence your incessant inner dialogue. Being peaceful isn't dependent on what your surroundings look like. It seldom has anything to do with what the people around you think, say or do. A noiseless environment isn't a requirement.

St. Francis's famous prayer states it better than I can: "Make me an instrument of Thy peace." In other words, St. Francis wasn't asking

God to provide him with peace. He was asking for guidance to be more like the peace he trusted was his Source. *Being peace* is different from *looking for peace.*

This principle isn't about merely choosing tranquil thoughts when you're feeling frayed and anxious. I suggest picturing a container deep within yourself out of which all your thoughts flow. Inside this container, at its very centre, imagine a candle flame. You need to make a commitment that this flame in the centre of the container holding all of your thoughts will never, ever even flicker, although the very worst may go before you. This is your container of peace, and only peaceful thoughts can fuel the burning candle. You don't need to change your thoughts as much as you need to learn to be an energy of peace lighting the way and attracting serene, harmonious thoughts and beings. In this way, you'll become a being of peace.

Obviously, you take this inner receptacle with you wherever you go. When people attempt to put some kind of pressure on you, when you feel overwhelmed, or when situations arise that previously incited your distress or bellicosity, you can immediately turn to your inner candle flame of peace and see how to keep your light glowing. This is *being* the peace that you wish for yourself. This is offering a matching vibration to your desire to be a tranquil and amicable being, rather than a person suffering from the disease of trying to make life go faster. You've already seen the results of that folly, and you notice the symptoms of stress in virtually everyone you meet.

As a being of peace, you make a huge impact on those around you. It's almost impossible to be totally stressed out in the presence of someone who has opted to *be peace*. Peace is a higher and faster energy—when you're being peace, just your presence alone will often nullify the uneasiness and tension in those around you. In fact, this state causes pheromones of measurable energy to emanate from you. They affect others, who become more peaceful without even being aware of the transformation taking place. The secret of this principle for restoring balance to your life is:

Be the peace and harmony you desire. You cannot get it from anything or anyone else.

So you're not ready to take Nisargadatta's profound advice and just be? Then work at *becoming* that being with the inner light of a steady candle flame. Here are some exercises to initiate becoming and being peaceful:

Want the Peace You Desire for
Yourself Even More for Others

Practise giving peace away wherever you go by imagining that only thoughts of peace are in the container within you. Offer these energies wherever possible. Become a peacemaker with your fellow workers, your family members, and especially those with whom you're in a love relationship. Leave your ego outside, where it can't extinguish your candle flame. Then offer someone with whom you usually argue and make wrong a new thought from the light: *You're making a good point; I'll think about that.* Or *Thanks for giving your opinion; I value what you have to say.* These statements may at first shock the recipient, but you know that you're practising becoming a being of peace by giving away what you want.

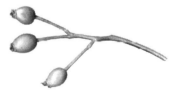

Ask

Use the words of St. Francis to ask to become peace: *Make me an instrument of Thy peace.* The act of asking, even if you don't feel an answer right away, will alter the balance toward becoming the peace that you desire. Once you've asked, you'll find that it is given more readily than you may have suspected. This is a process of suspending your ego and allowing the higher, more spiritually based energies to weigh in toward your becoming more balanced.

Slow Down

Take your time. I urge you to reproduce Ramakrishna's and Bertrand Russell's quotes that are at the beginning of this chapter. Post them where you constantly notice them and let them become a part of your being. Your work isn't terribly important... your worldly duties aren't terribly important... Make your first and primary priority in your life *being in balance with the Source of Creation*. Become thoughtful in your slowed-down time, and invite the Divine to be known in your life. Being the peace you desire means becoming a relaxed person whose balance point doesn't attract anxiety and stress symptoms.

Make deliberate, conscious efforts to slow yourself down by relaxing your mind. Take a little more time to enjoy your life here on this planet: Be more contemplative by noticing the stars, the clouds, the rivers, the animals, the rainstorms, and all of the natural world. And then extend the same slowed-down loving energy to all people. Begin with your family—take a few extra hours to romp with your children, to listen to their ideas, to read them a story. Go for a walk with your most cherished loved one and say how much you treasure him or her in your life.

Extend this slowed-down perspective outward at work, in your community, and even to strangers. Make a deliberate effort to give someone your place in line rather than hurrying to be first. Become conscious of your efforts to become the peace you desire and to live in balance, even while you're driving. As you slow your thoughts down and decide to enjoy your life more, bring your car to a stop at an amber caution light rather than speeding on through. Consciously drive at a relaxed pace rather than in a frenzy to get some-where two minutes sooner. Let other people into the stream of traffic by being courteous rather than right.

These are all ways to begin the process of realignment. Become conscious of your desire to be at peace, and then match your present-moment thoughts to that desire. You'll become more compassionate without trying to be, simply because you've aligned your inner world with your desire to be in balance. You'll find that your body will feel more in balance as you pursue this glorious quest, as it will experience fewer symptoms of stress. Your body weight will adjust to the optimal level as you return to a state of perfect equilibrium. Your skin will reflect the balance and peace that you're becoming. Your digestion will return to normal without the aid of pills. Your sleep patterns will adjust. Your bowels will function perfectly as they were designed to. In short, you will be in perfect balance.

You will not only be in balance, but, irony of ironies, you'll become more productive! You'll have more abundance flowing in your life while being peaceful for the first time since you were a child. Take the advice of my teacher Nisargadatta Maharaj: *Just be!*

Give it a try, and I promise that you'll be peacefully surprised.

Chapter Three

You Can't Kiss Your Own Ear

(Balancing How You See Yourself with What You Project to the World)

Chapter Three

The opening quote from Theodore Roosevelt is both compelling and filled with irony. Your balance point is often found in feedback from those whose opinions you trust and respect. This is an exceptionally valuable option to give yourself. Being concerned with just your own personal assessment of your behaviours or actions, at the expense of what others think, can cause you to be out of balance. I'm not advocating that opinions or criticism, or even praise from others, in any way immobilize, upset, or flatter you. Too much emphasis on what others think can mean that praise or criticism is part of the package tipping the scale toward imbalance. What follows is a personal example to illustrate what I mean.

I vividly recall my very first year teaching as a college professor in the summer session at Wayne State University in 1970. A small group of graduate students was making a presentation to the class as a part of their final course requirements. I repeatedly heard twitters and outright laughter at some of the antics of the presenting group, and I sat there, mystified by what was so funny. Finally, as more and more of the students looked in my direction to see my reaction to the presentation, it hit me like a ton of bricks: They were imitating me! One student had pulled his belt down to expose a dour-postured protruding gut sticking out above the belt. Others in the group spoke in excessively loud voices and gesticulated wildly, all the while making indecipherable marks on the chalkboard.

And there I sat, watching *myself* being portrayed good-naturedly, in a manner that was in total contrast to how I saw myself and what I was projecting to the world. That little episode still sticks with me more than 35 years later. It was almost immediately after that experience that I made a deliberate decision to permanently get rid of that protruding gut and get into optimal physical shape. I also learned the hard way, by being the target of a spoof, how to be a less dogmatic teacher in the classroom.

We can actually learn a lot about how we're being perceived by others if we're able to assimilate the input. It's been my experience, particularly in helping to raise eight children, that there's often a huge imbalance between how we see ourselves and how we're perceived by the rest of the world. Becoming aware of this disparity can be extremely helpful in leading a more fulfilling and balanced life. You certainly don't want to base your entire existence upon how pleasing you are to those around you. A balanced individual, however, is free to make the choice to change something if they're comfortable with feedback that may be unflattering.

What This Imbalance Looks Like

Perhaps the most important question in this regard is: *How do you want to be perceived in this world?* Anyone who responds that they don't care at all is trying to live with blinkers on—a rather unbalanced style, to be sure. Of course you care! In some cases, your very livelihood depends on your response to this question. You want to enjoy relating in a joyful, playful, intimate, loving, helpful, concerned, caring and thoughtful manner with others. It's the nature of all of our human relationships to want to give and receive those emotions, and to feel connected to each other.

If you also desire spiritual consciousness, then you need to be more in harmony with your spiritual Source. This is a Source of love, kindness, joy, beauty, nonjudgment, creativity and endless abundance. If you think that you personify all of these qualities, yet everyone else perceives you in a totally different light, then it's likely that you're living an illusion and will continue to be in a state of imbalance.

The answer to how you want to be perceived in the world is, at its simplest: *I want to be seen as a truthful person.* You want the truth of who you believe you are to mesh with what you're projecting outward. If this is unsuccessful, you're aware of it, even if you opt to ignore it. The imbalance surfaces in your daily interactions, showing up in feelings of being upset, out of sorts, confused, and often misunderstood. *My intentions are good, so why is it that no one else sees it this way?* and *I try to be a good employee, father, citizen and husband, but I always seem to be misconstrued or mis-judged.* This results in a continual state of frustration and even anger. Your anxious or saddened emotional state says: *I know I'm a good person with good intentions, but no one else seems to realize this.*

You need to make a decision to realign yourself on an energetic basis to get the scales balanced between your idealized self and your realized self, as perceived by the majority of people in your life.

Restoring the Balance
Through Realignment

When you balance the way you want to be with the way you're being received, there's a distinctly pleasurable feeling of being in harmony with life. It's not that you're seeking approval or grovelling for respect or love. It's more that you're in the world in a way that's congruent with your inner desire to be the kind of person you are.

You accomplish this by first noticing when you're feeling misperceived, then determining if your words and actions match the truth of your inner thoughts. This alignment check will eventually and almost automatically give you a reading that compares what you're projecting outwardly with what you're inwardly wanting to express. Let's take a look at some of these indices, keeping in mind that every thought you have about yourself has an energetic component.

Here are some of the most obvious qualities that describe the ways you feel about yourself. Review these elements, keeping in mind that your objective is to balance what you send out in your daily interactions and behaviours with the truth within you. This alignment check calls for self-honesty along with a willingness to experience radical humility in the process.

— **I am a loving human being.** If you both desire and believe this to be true about yourself, then you're two-thirds of the way toward being in balance in this principle. Your desire to be a loving person, and at the same time your truth that you *are* a loving person, leave only the third element: how others perceive you. If you're feeling misunderstood or unloved, then before you can perfectly balance the scales, you need to determine whether the loving human being you see yourself as, and want to be, is seen by others.

Here are some ways of being that are counterproductive to being perceived as a loving human being and that create an imbalance:

- A strong position of hatred toward anyone or any group of people— you're out of balance.

- Violence in any form, including aggressive verbal outbursts—you're out of balance.

- Support for weapons designed to produce megadeath explosions—you're out of balance.

- You enjoy being entertained by films portraying hatred and killing—you're out of balance.

- Verbally belittling others' beliefs and insisting that your beliefs are superior—you're out of balance.

    In order to realign yourself to create the

balance you desire, seek the feedback of significant people in your life. Ask them if you come across as the loving human being you believe yourself to be. Then begin the process of monitoring your thoughts to see how they line up with your self-portrait. And finally, let your thoughts of love become the driving force behind your unloving behaviours. This is true alignment.

Begin looking at the world as a vast mirror reflecting back to you exactly what you are. If you truly are a loving human being, the world will look like a loving place to you, and this will be how you're perceived. You will have restored balance, and consequently there will be no discrepancy between how you see yourself and what the world is reflecting back to you. If the world continues to look like an unloving and unlivable place, I urge you to keep examining the kind of energy that you're projecting outward.

— **I am a kind human being.** You cannot be kind to me and unkind to your waiter... and be in balance. When you persistently extend arrogance outward in the direction of other people, even if you feel justified in your actions, that's how you're perceived and defined. You need to know that you're not coming across as a balanced, kind person.

You may indeed exemplify kindness in how you treat your children and your grand-mother, and even all of the children and all of the grandmothers of the world. But if you honk your horn in red-faced anger at a slow-driving grand-mother who's taking her grandchildren to school, then you're way, way, way out of balance. The discrepancy between your own idealized self and how others perceive you is vast, and it will create a real sense of imbalance within you that can manifest as a personality disorder. You know that you aren't living up to what you say about yourself, and other people are pointing it out more and more frequently.

You're the only person responsible for the decision to generate a vibrational match to your desire to be seen as a kind human being, and you can begin to notice when you feel out of sync with that desire: You can cancel an unkind thought in midstream and decide in an instant to be harmonious. You can stop yourself at the moment you're cursing somebody and elevate your thoughts to kindness. If you see yourself as desirous of being a kind person, then consciously spend time daily aligning your thoughts with your desire. The Universe will cooperate, bringing you more and more of the same kindness.

— **I am a joyful, happy human being.** In this category, your feelings are the measurement you need to pay attention to. In fact, they require your undivided attention. Do you feel good most of the time, or are you a person who looks for occasions to be offended? Do you feel happy and content, or are you easily outraged over the misconduct of others? Does your joy turn quickly to despair when you read the newspaper or listen to the news? Do people around you really think that you're a happy camper in your daily life? Do you regularly hear others telling you to "lighten up" or "chill out" and "stop letting yourself get so worked up"? These are clues indicating the balance or imbalance between how you see yourself and what you project to others. The alignment check for this principle involves noticing your feelings and your ability to sustain them, along with feedback from people you trust.

You're a joyful person if you live from joy, extend joy wherever possible, and if those around you feel joyful in your presence. Here are some suggestions to restore balance in this principle:

- Make a commitment to look for joy everywhere.

- Offer joyful commentary wherever possible.

- Reach out to others in cheerfulness, even if you initially have to fake it.

- Go on a rampage of appreciation, rather then discussing the evils of the world.

- Use every opportunity to radiate joy.

If you can let joy be your habitual way of responding to the world, you'll restore balance on the scale of how you see yourself and how others perceive your attitude of gratitude for life. If you project energy that results in others feeling threatened, uncomfortable and not wanting to be around you, then you're simply out of balance. If you're unclear about your effect on others, take an inventory of those who are willing to be honest with you, and discover how your self-perception matches up with their input.

— **I am a nonjudgmental human being**. If you're truly nonjudgmental, then it will be impossible for you to categorize or generalize individuals into groups such as: old, uneducated, teenyboppers, conservatives, liberals, and so on. A stereotype is a judgment—you cannot be non-judgmental and be critical of the different ways people talk, eat, dress, socialize, dance, or anything else. If you believe that you're nonjudgmental but admit that you have a tendency to generalize and criticize, then you're out of balance! You're due for a realignment so that your current thoughts, and ultimately your behaviours, will become a vibrational match to your inner self-portrait.

Make a conscious decision to look for what is right and pleasing in others. Create a new habit of complimenting those around you. Decide that you're going to disregard stereotypes, and refuse to engage in conversations that dwell on judging anyone. Turn judgments into blessings to restore the imbalance between how you want to be and how you're actually presenting yourself to the world.

If you want to be a nonjudgmental person and associate with others at this level, I suggest that you shift to a state of awe and bewilderment as you appreciate the beauty that's in all people and all things. Stop your habitual way of noticing what you *don't* like, and instead look hard and deliberately for what you find pleasing. Then articulate what you've discovered as a way to reinforce the new habit of being unconditionally accepting.

Even if your judgments are nothing more than thoughts, I urge you to change those thoughts immediately upon recognizing them. If you see an obese person and think, *He's disgusting,* you're aligning with a point of attraction that attracts disgust. Rebalance this energy by sending a silent blessing to the person. On the nonjudgmental side of the balance scale, think about how much love and support this person could use. I guarantee that you'll feel the difference internally, and at the same time feel more compassionately connected to that individual. The energy of nonjudgment is totally balanced, as opposed to the energy of contempt, pity, or some other negative opinion.

Become aware of all of your behaviours and feelings. Then attempt to determine if they match your vision of yourself, and if that self-image is what others see. You'll immediately feel discord when you discover imbalance, and that's when you can choose to change habits to match your desires and restore equilibrium to your life.

D. H. Lawrence once observed: "What you intuitively desire, that is possible to you." I couldn't agree more. However, you must repeatedly ask yourself, *Does my intuitive desire match up with what I give to the world?* When it does, balance is restored, and self-fulfilment is your reward.

Chapter Four

*Your Addictions Tell You,
"You'll Never Get Enough
of What You Don't Want"*

*(Balancing Your Desire
for What You Want
with Your Addictive
Behaviour)*

Chapter Four

If I were to rate the nine habits discussed in this book, this one might get the prize for being the most unbelievable: *spending our precious life energy chasing after something we don't want, and never getting enough of whatever it is that we're relentlessly pursuing!* Fortunately, this is one imbalance that's relatively easy to correct, despite all we've been told about the difficulties involved in conquering addictions. The concept of *fighting* and *conquering* addiction is the wrong approach—I believe that we need to begin by removing those words from our vocabulary. Martin Luther King, Jr. once remarked that the only way to convert an enemy to a friend is through love, not hatred or fighting.

We Don't Conquer Anything, and There's Nothing to Fight

Consider the results we've achieved when we've tried to fight something in order to conquer it. For example, ever since war was declared on poverty, there's more of it in the world than ever. Our wars on drugs have only served to triple our prison populations and bring illegal substances to more people at younger ages. (As early as junior high school, there's hardly a child who doesn't know how to acquire all manner of drugs.) Our wars on crime have resulted in more criminals, more fear, more surveillance, more distrust, and more abuse by law-enforcement personnel. Our war on terror has turned us into people who behave toward those we label *terrorists* in ways that emulate the terrorism we're supposedly desirous of eliminating. When war was officially declared on Iraq, America became more hated, and the number of people signing up to become suicide bombers multiplied dramatically. And our wars on cancer, obesity, and hunger have not eliminated those conditions either.

Here's the reasoning behind what I've just elaborated: The truth of this Universe is that we live in an energy system that operates on the Law of Attraction. That is, we become what we think about all day long. If we think about what we hate, this is an energy that we're offering to our desires. In this system, then, we'll attract more of what we think about. Consequently, more of what we hate is what we will attract. We act on our thoughts: our thoughts of hate, violence, fighting, and war generate actions of hate, violence, fighting, and war. And lo and behold, we see the fruits of this thinking showing up even if our intentions are positively aligned with God energy. We get what we think about, whether we want it or not.

Thoughts that translate into fighting and war almost always guarantee that the response is a counterforce—that is, others will respond in kind to our desire to fight and conquer. This kind of force/counterforce can continue for centuries, with unborn generations programmed to carry on the fight.

This same understanding of how fighting weakens us and generates more imbalance in our lives is applicable to our experience with addictions. We can become addiction-free relatively quickly if we make a decision to eliminate fighting and conquering from our efforts. The thoughts and energy that replace fighting need to be in the form of nonwarlike thoughts. As Emerson said so succinctly: "The remedy of all blunders, the cure of blindness, the cure of crime, is love..." And addictions constitute one huge blunder, I can assure you, having spent a great deal of my own life immersed in such folly.

Overcoming Blunder-Filled Thinking

For those of you who may not be familiar with my friend Ram Dass, in the late 1960s he helped shape the awakening consciousness of an entire generation with his bestseller *Be Here Now.*

One of my favorite Ram Dass stories is the one he tells about an early encounter with Neem Karoli Baba, his guru in India. Ram Dass brought some capsules with him to India that were designed to dramatically alter one's state of consciousness. Neem Karoli Baba confronted Ram Dass about these pills and asked him to give all of them to him. Ram Dass thought that he'd brought a long-term supply of this very powerful psychedelic substance—yet he watched in horror and amazement as this enlightened being swallowed all of them right before his eyes, with no visible reaction. His guru then asked him if he had any more, since these obviously weren't working. After telling this story, Ram Dass concluded with one of his most sagacious observations: "If you're already in Detroit," he observed, "then you don't have to take a bus to get there."

Addictions of every description are vehicles that people board in order to get someplace higher, more pleasurable, more peaceful, more tuned in and turned on, and so on. But if you're already aligned with this energy, then it's obviously unnecessary to climb aboard any vehicle headed to a place where you currently reside.

I've played with addictions and addictive behaviours for a large part of my life. In fact, I'd say that these various addictions have been among my greatest teachers, allowing me to see that there's a higher level of consciousness and blissful awareness available to us all. But I'm also aware that using substances of non-wellbeing in order to experience this separate reality is assuredly a counterfeit means of doing so.

The pattern goes something like this: We must have more and more of what we desire. The more of it we take or imbibe, the more we need. The less effective it is as we consume more. Then, to top off this huge imbalance, what we're using to get to this place of bliss is toxic to our well being! The addiction is increasing our imbalance.

Our desire is for bliss, peace, love, health, freedom and so on, but the addictive behaviour gives us precisely the opposite. If it goes unchecked, it will wreak havoc on our body and mind, and ultimately destroy us.

I'm essentially addiction-free, and I want you to know that I didn't get to this place by fighting my addictive nature. In fact, the more I tried to conquer addictions at various stages of my life to things such as sugar, soda pop, caffeine, nicotine, alcohol, and certain drugs, the more they'd gain a foothold on me. *Force/counterforce*: I'd apply my weapons, and they'd bring out their artillery, with my body as the battleground where the war was being waged. I was blundering my way into deeper addiction. Earlier, I quoted Ralph Waldo

Emerson, who said: "The remedy of all blunders
… is love." How would things be different if we
followed his advice? The two key words are
blunder and *love*. Let's examine them more closely.

— **Blunder.** Why call an addiction a
blunder? Demanding more and more of something your body and mind vehemently despise is
addiction. Choosing the lopsided world of addiction
over the equilibrium that is your spiritual heritage
is a major distortion of your birthright. When
you do that, you're mismanaging this life. This is
something I strongly believe is a blunder that can
be balanced with love.

You originated from an invisible spiritual
energy field of pure wellbeing. Your desire is to be

balanced in that spirit in your thoughts and behaviours—now, in this life, in this moment, in your bodily form. You want that harmony, and sense that it's available without having to leave your body, or in other words, die. So, in that interpretation, you're seeking a balance that allows you to die while you're alive.

You'll return to spirit, the non-form, upon your death, but you have the option of choosing to live in true enlightened balance, or God-realization... now, in this physical state. Your Source doesn't create from toxicity. It doesn't fill your veins or your stomach or any part of you with poison or excess. It creates from wellbeing, balance and effortless perfection. This is your spiritual heritage.

And love can correct the blunders that distance you from your spiritual self.

— **Love.** Why is love the antidote to addictions? It's very simple—because love is what you are; it's the centre of your creation. It's your point of origination and can become your point of attraction as well. As Karl Menninger told his patients, and anyone else who was suffering and willing to listen, "Love cures, the ones who receive love and the ones who give it, too." In transcending your addictive habits, you have the opportunity to be both the giver and the receiver of the spiritual balm of love. As you apply it, you feel the balance returning to your life. You no longer pursue a counterfeit freedom, and you no longer attract what you don't want. Instead, you seek the balance of being connected to your authentic nature.

Reconnection to Wellbeing

Our proclivity toward addictive behaviours subsides measurably as we begin to practise reconnecting to our Source of being. Many books have been written on the subject of overcoming addictions. There are countless rehabilitation programmes and centres to help those who are caught in the grip of drugs, alcohol, food, caffeine, sex, gambling, or something else that fits the description of chasing after what we don't want.

I support any programme designed to help people escape this unbalanced cycle that is such a destroyer of lives. My contribution here is a brief description of the key points I've found extremely useful in becoming an addiction-free person. The following five thoughts helped interrupt my out-of-balance thinking and behaviour. Practised with honesty and integrity, they can contribute to a new sense of empowerment and wellbeing that allows you to be free of unwanted addictions.

1. It's All about Realignment

This is number one because when you really practise it, you never want to pursue what you don't want at the expense of what you do want. You long to be in harmony, and you desire wellbeing. You came from wellbeing, so you simply need to choose thoughts that align with that foundation to find your way back into alignment.

Practise praying silently as a steady background whenever and wherever you can. Personalize and vary prayers such as this example derived from the St. Francis Prayer: *Make me an instrument of Thy wellbeing.* See yourself always summoning the energy of wellbeing from your spiritual Source. Think like an animal who would never think of pursuing what it doesn't want. Why don't birds chase after butterflies? Because they're poisonous. Ever heard of a robin in therapy trying to overcome its desire to eat butterflies? Silly, yes, but it's a helpful image to hook onto.

So think like a human being with wellbeing. Eventually you'll think like the Divine soul that you are, and you'll be in vibrational harmony with the wellbeing that is your very nature.

2. Love Your
Addictions

If it's food, love it. If it's cocaine, love it. If it's painkillers, love them. If it's cigarettes, love them. These are some of your greatest teachers. They've taught you through direct experience what it is that you no longer wish to be. They've taken you to the depths for some reason. This is an intelligent system you're a part of. There are no accidents in a Universe supported by omniscience and omnipotence. Be grateful for these teachers.

If you hate them, curse them, and attempt to fight these addictions, you tip the balance toward hatred and fighting. You then continue to chase after what you don't want because you're in a weakened state. Fighting weakens; love empowers.

So tip the scale toward love. Be grateful for the addictions that have taught you so much. Send them a silent blessing. By doing so, you shift toward the love that you are.

3. Love Yourself

This is the natural outgrowth of choosing to love your addictions. Think of your body as a sacred temple, and extend reverence as a form of love. Be aware of, and grateful for, every organ, every drop of blood, every appendage, and every cell that constitutes your body. Start right this minute by offering a silent prayer of gratitude for your liver, your heart, and your brain. Just say: *Thank you, God, for this glorious gift. I treasure it, and with Your help, today I will begin the process of loving it unconditionally.* If you still feel attracted to substances that you despise, say this silent prayer before ingesting them. Love will ultimately become the added weight that rebalances your life.

One of my favorite American poets, Henry W. Longfellow, tells us: "He that respects himself is safe from others; he wears a coat of mail that none can pierce." When we truly respect and love ourselves, it's as if we have a shield of flexible armour made of metal rings and loops of chain that protects us from the addictive *other* that's been a part of our life.

4. Remove All Shame

You've done nothing wrong. You haven't failed—you've only produced results. The question isn't about how bad you've been; it's about what you intend to do with the results you've produced. If you opt for shame and guilt, you choose the one emotional reaction that will disempower you more than any other. Whatever your present-moment status in relation to your addictions, it's all perfect. You had to go through the traumas you went through. You had to disappoint the people you've mistreated. You had to get this far down. You needed this out-of-balance energy in order to aid you in generating the energy to get you to the higher place where you're now headed.

You are still a Divine being in the eyes of God, despite any weaknesses that you feel are incongruous with God's love. You needed all of those experiences, and now that you're contemplating leaving them behind and rejoining your spiritual Source of wellbeing, shame will only hamper you and send you back to that absurdly unbalanced world where you never get enough of what you don't want.

5. Live from a New Knowing

Finally, create a space within yourself, somewhere very private that only you and God are privy to. In this inner space, post the words *I know*. This is your invisible connection to God, where purity and wellbeing define your new addiction-free self. Regardless of how many people distrust you and remind you of how many times in the past you've failed to live up to your promises, this is your space of knowing.

From this unshakable space, ask for Divine guidance. Ask to have the ecstatic energy of purity and wellbeing flow directly to your heart. If you slip, retreat immediately to this space of knowing. Forgive yourself and see yourself surrounded by

God's love, holding you in balance once again. As a man who has been there, I can promise you that you'll be provided with all of the guidance, direction, and strength that you need—and you'll get what you do want rather than what you do not want.

Overcoming the imbalance of addictive thinking begins and ends with your awareness that you, with the help of your Source, have everything you need right now to end your imbalance. As an ancient Hindu saying reminds us, "God gives food to every bird, but He doesn't throw it into the nest." Realign with God, and fly without the weight of addiction. I promise you that being in balance and free of addiction is much more exhilarating!

Chapter Five

You're Not What
You Eat; You're What You
Believe about What You Eat

(Balancing Your Desire to Have Your Body Feel Great,
with What You Feed
It and How You
Exercise It)

Chapter Five

Your beliefs reflect the current relative state of health that your body is in, just as much as your diet and exercise regimen do. If you desire a gloriously healthy body but behave in unwholesome ways, you're obviously going to be out of balance. But even more telling are the kinds of thoughts and beliefs that you have about your health.

Obviously, just like everyone else, you want to have perfect health. So let's put this idealistic wish at the top rung of an imaginary ten-step ladder. There, at the apex of your desires regarding your health, is this longing for a body that's healthy and feels great. Now, visualize this ten-rung ladder with these two questions in mind.

1. At what rung of the ladder are your *behaviours* in relation to your tenth-rung desire?

2. At what rung of the ladder are your *beliefs about your behaviours* in relation to your tenth-rung desire?

I'd make a calculated guess that anyone who's overweight, and so out of shape that walking up a few flights of stairs leaves them breathless, is contributing second-rung energies to tenth-rung desires. In other words, they're way out of balance. The same is true for people with any number of physical maladies attributable to lifestyle, such as ulcers, high blood pressure, indigestion, palpitations of the heart and so on.

To create a balance where you can honestly say that your body is enjoying its optimal level of health and that you're grateful to live in such a glorious House of God means making some new decisions around the two questions I've posed. It may be surprising to read that I'm not suggesting a radical change in diet or advocating that you embark on an exercise programme designed for a bodybuilder or a marathon runner (although these are distinct possibilities). No, I'm suggesting a radical realignment in the energy of the beliefs you give to the tenth-rung desire.

If you're overweight, out of shape and suffering unnecessarily from physical maladies that are related to your lifestyle, this radical idea may require a lot of determination to overcome your disbelief. So begin right now by rereading the title of this chapter. Isn't it strange to think that your diet or lack of exercise aren't completely responsible for the state of your health? Maybe it has to do with what you *believe*.

The second quote at the beginning of this chapter was written by the author of *Zorba the Greek*. Zorba is one of the most passionate fictional characters ever created, housed in a body that wasn't a bodybuilder's dream. Nikos Kazantzakis encourages us to practise believing passionately, because out of that belief the desire will be created.

Your tenth-rung desire to enjoy living in a healthy body will manifest when you sufficiently desire it. And this is precisely how you can correct the imbalance that has one end weighted down to the ground by behaviours and beliefs that are diametrically opposed to what you desire.

Rebalancing Your Health by Realigning Your Beliefs

Deepak Chopra, my friend and colleague of many years, once observed: "Your brain produces a chemical that relays the news of your happiness to all 52 million of your body cells—who rejoice and join in." So picture yourself as you're about to enjoy a hot-fudge sundae or a piece of birthday cake: Are you happy, or are you filled with guilt and apprehension before you take your first bite? And what beliefs have you attached yourself to that are preventing your brain from producing and relaying good news to the rest of your body, including those that are about to be converted to unhappy fat cells rather than happy healthy cells?

As difficult as it may be for you to accept, your beliefs about what you're eating and how you're living your life are far more important to examine and change than the actual activities of eating and exercising. The mind-body connection has clearly been established in medical and scientific research. Your beliefs are thoughts, and your thoughts are energy. If you've convinced yourself that what you're about to do is going to have a deleterious effect on your body, then you're doing precisely what Kazantzakis suggests— you're passionately believing in something that still does not exist. That is, your unhealthy bodily reaction to what you're about to do is only a thought, not a material reality. However, by holding on to that thought, you facilitate the process of indeed making it your material reality.

Now suppose that you decide to passionately believe in something that doesn't yet exist, and that something is *you* in a perfectly healthy body composed entirely of the wellbeing that characterized it when it materialized into a physical soul. Moreover, you include a belief that your body is capable of converting any fuel that it receives into healthy, happy cells—a radical idea, perhaps, because so many people believe something to the contrary. Nevertheless, you passionately decide to believe this, even though the reality doesn't yet exist.

As you adopt the idea that your brain and body are more than capable of converting any fuel into healthy, happy cells, you begin the process of looking around for evidence that supports your belief, rather than attaching yourself to contrary, non-health-producing belief systems. *Yes, you now say, there are many people who get what they want, when they want; and who pay no attention to diets, who don't obsessively weigh themselves every day, and who are not only at a normal weight, but are happy in their own skin. I'm going to think like they do for a while and see if it works.*

As you engage in this radically new idea, guess what begins to happen? You actually begin to alter your eating behaviours. Why? Because eating healthy food in smaller portions feels good, and feeling good is what your tenth-rung desire is all about.

But it has to start with a thought that feels good, and it is this: *Whatever I eat is okay. I'll instruct my brain and my body chemistry to convert whatever I eat into health.* You have a whole new cycle of thinking to examine, and this new way of thinking passionately about something that still doesn't exist applies to being physically in shape as well.

Shaping Up Your Out-of-Balance Thinking

So what are your beliefs about what it takes to be in shape and physically healthy? Is it necessary for a person to suffer every day and go through a rigorous workout routine in order to be in good health physically? These are commonly held beliefs that should be challenged if you're seeking a more balanced life. Your wish is for a body that looks and feels terrific—that's the tenth-rung desire.

So what kind of thoughts do you entertain in order to reach this desire? All too often your thoughts go something like this: *I'm not an active person. It doesn't matter how much I exercise—I still can't get the weight off and get in shape. I hate running and sweating. I'm not destined to be athletic.* These beliefs, and many like them, keep you on the bottom rungs of that ladder. Moreover, they contribute enormously to the obesity crisis, and to the existence of so much lifestyle-related disease that originates in this kind of collective thinking.

When you change your thoughts, and what you believe about what's possible for you, you change everything, including your physiology. You need to fervently believe that you're a specimen of perfect health by creating that picture of yourself as looking and feeling great. Carrying this image wherever you go and believing passionately in its reality is a total thought-changer!

Now the inner dialogue will sound more like this: *I'm headed in the direction of perfect health. I have no shame or guilt about myself or my behaviour. If I choose to be a couch potato, I'll be a healthy, trim, beautiful couch potato. I love my body. I'm going to take great care of it because it houses the sacred being that I am.* As you begin this new ritual of changing the way you look at your body, the body that you're looking at will change.

You've been immersed in a culture that promotes how you should feel about your body, based on commercial endeavours that want to realize profits from your dissatisfaction with yourself. The sales pitch is that if you don't look like a supermodel, you should feel some remorse. Right there we have the beginnings of eating disorders, obesity and weakened physical constitutions. When you buy into this kind of collective brainwashing, you set yourself up for a great imbalance between your desire to have a healthy body that feels great, and daily self-defeating behaviours leading to ill health and feeling exhausted and out of shape.

Remember that you become what you think about. Why think of yourself in any way that leads to less-than-perfect health? What's the point in looking at your body in its current condition of disrepair and taking on a set of beliefs guaranteed to make matters worse?

Here's a radically new option for you. Believe passionately in what doesn't yet exist, and recall Kazantzakis's observation that "the nonexistent is whatever we have not sufficiently desired". You can adopt a belief system that's so well-balanced that no one, and not any social pressure, can weigh it down or put it out of range of your self-love and reverence for the sacred temple that is your body. Then you can experience what it feels like to passionately believe in something that doesn't yet exist. That new belief system is going to be the balance point allowing you to enjoy a friendly, loving, healthy relationship with your body, and alter any self-sabotaging behaviour.

Acting on Your New Passionate Belief in Something That Doesn't Exist... Yet!

As your beliefs go, so goes your behaviour. When you're able to see yourself as a Divine creation who emanated from a Source of pure unconditional love, with a total absence of shame or self-repudiation, your body has no choice but to enjoy the trip. Whatever you decide to eat, if your thoughts are: *It's my intention that this food be converted to energy that will make my body feel vigorous and strong*, your body will begin to respond in kind. Once you remove the old beliefs that fostered feeling anxious, guilty, worried, and even fearful, your brain begins producing chemicals that return you to a balance of feeling good and creating a healthy body.

Yes, I'm saying that by reprogramming your thinking to align with your desire to be and feel healthy, you can and will alter the unhealthy behaviours that produced ill health and being out of balance. This is a function of law. Here's how William James, the father of modern psychology, put it:

There is a law in psychology that if you form a picture in your mind of what you would like to be, and you keep and you hold that picture there long enough, you will soon become exactly as you have been thinking.

Such is the awesome power of our thoughts. But I'm also saying something that goes beyond this idea of your body acting automatically in response to your reprogrammed thinking. As you begin to balance stereotypical expectations for your body that are out of harmony with your desire to be healthy and feel great, you'll notice another automatic reaction: Your behaviours will begin to spontaneously seek to balance with your expressed desires.

It may happen gradually, but there it is — you see yourself not living in fear or overly focused on your appearance. This wonderful awareness of self-acceptance combines with a strong desire to treat your body with respect. Your eating habits shift without making a conscious decision to change anything. You stop counting calories and simply enjoy what you're eating, knowing that you can trust the inherent spiritual wisdom that's programmed into your DNA, your connection to the Source that created the baby you once were.

You've found a better way to balance and enjoy your life by trusting your thoughts to attract the health you desire. You're able to relax and enjoy this journey. By consciously having Spirit weigh in through the energy of your thoughts, you've tipped the balance in favour of your desires. Your ego, which identifies with your body, has been relegated to a less dominant role. Spirit has no excess fat, indigestion, hunger pangs or overeating habits, and this is where you're now choosing to make your stand.

You're choosing thoughts that are in harmony with your originating Spirit, and in so doing there's no room for being unhealthy. Because you're more at peace in your thoughts, believing that whatever you do can be converted to a healthy reaction, you take on the same automatic new response in your approach to exercise and physical wellbeing. Your newly balanced internal-picturing procedure affirms William James's assertion.

I am a Divinely healthy and fit human being. Think it! Say it! Believe it! Even if you've harboured a previous image of being overweight and out of shape, say it anyway. You're starting the process of passionately believing in something that still doesn't exist. By affirming it and making it your inner reality, you'll activate a new automatic response that resonates with your stated desire. The next thing you know, you'll be going for a walk. Then perhaps you'll participate in something that has definitely not been part of the balance in your life up till now—maybe a jog, a yoga class or a health-club membership. This will all happen without trying, because you must act upon your beliefs.

The imbalance between your desire for a healthy body that feels great and persistently unhealthy habits is not remedied by simply changing those habits. You must have a firm determination to learn the art of passionately believing in something that doesn't yet exist, and refuse to allow that picture to be distorted by you or anyone else. Truly, you are not what you eat or how much you exercise, but rather what you believe about the you that you're presently birthing in your thoughts.

Keep reminding yourself: *I get what I think about, whether I want it or not.*

Chapter Six

*You Can't Discover Light
by Analyzing the Darkness*

*(Balancing Your Desire for Prosperity
with Your Habits of Scarcity)*

Chapter Six

If you had to search for light, the one thing you'd obviously shun would be the darkness. You'd know for certain that spending your time analyzing dark places and wallowing around blindly in the dark wouldn't be the way to discover and experience the light. Now exchange the words *light* and *dark* in this example for the words *abundance* and *scarcity*—the same logic should now apply. You can't find abundance by analyzing and wallowing around in scarcity consciousness. Yet this is often why a disparity exists between your desire for prosperity and the lack of it in your life.

Review the observation offered by Ernest Holmes in the quote at the beginning of this chapter: "As we express life, we fulfill God's law of abundance..." Think of this as a legally binding dictum from God, as a law. Even St. Paul observed that "God is able to provide you with every blessing in abundance." I draw the conclusion that prosperity is something that's always available, because this is descriptive of the Source from which we originated. If we came from unlimited abundance, then we must be what we came from.

Scarcity isn't a problem because of where you were born or what your parents accumulated or the state of the economy. The so-called problem of scarcity is due to the simple fact that you tipped your belief away from your original connection to unlimited abundance and began to live in and analyze scarcity—the equivalent of darkness in the first paragraph of this chapter. I advocate making a shift toward analyzing the light of prosperity and correcting this imbalance between what you desire and the way you're living.

How You Avoid Expressing Life and Fail to Fulfil God's Law of Abundance

In order to express life and be the recipient of God's blessing of abundance, you need to know when you have thoughts and behaviours that unbalance your desires. The voice of your balance position is something I've repeatedly written about in this book: *You become what you think about all day long.*

Here's a list of out-of-balance-type situations:

- Dwelling on what's missing from your life.

- Conversations that are heavily weighted with what's lacking in your life.

- Complaining to whomever will listen about all of the reasons you've been prevented from having more.

- Cultivating an inner picture of yourself as a person who's just plain unlucky.

These ways of thinking and being set into motion an energy pattern that attracts precisely what you activate into your life. If you think scarcity, you'll create scarcity. If you talk to others about your lack, you'll just attract more lack. If you analyze your shortages, then more shortages will appear!

I'm aware that this may seem simplistic — that is, *just change your thinking and money will come flying in your window!* But before dismissing this, consider that an out-of-balance existence is asking you to notice what barriers and resistance you've erected in a world where God is available to provide you with all blessings in abundance.

Removing Your Resistance

Your desire to attract prosperity represents a highly spiritual request. It's perfectly attuned to the law of abundance from which you originated. Your imbalances are energies in the form of thoughts that you mistakenly believe will bring about the desired prosperity.

Following are seven of the most common thoughts that make the manifestation of prosperity virtually impossible. I call these the *unmagnificent seven*, because each belief practically guarantees that you'll stay stuck in scarcity in the way that Ayn Rand describes in the quote at the beginning of this chapter. The *degree to which you think* is the determining factor in creating a life of prosperity.

So here are the seven thought systems that keep you out of balance:

1. It's Not God's Will

By blaming God for not having what you need or desire, you justify a built-in excuse for accepting your lot in life. In reality, as St. Paul reminds us, God is more than willing to provide you with the blessing of abundance. In fact, God is pure abundance, but *you're* the one out of balance on the prosperity scale. By putting the responsibility for your shortages on Divine will, you create enormous resistance energetically. You're asking the Universe to send you more of what you believe in.

The solution to removing this barrier (which applies to all seven of these resistance energies) is changing the belief. Carlos Castaneda, writing in *Journey to Ixtlan*, said: "If I really felt that my spirit was distorted I should simply fix it—purge it, make it perfect—because there was no other task in our entire lives which was more worthwhile."

How do you "fix it," "purge it," and "make it perfect"? By first catching yourself in the midst of a fallacious thought, and replacing that thought with something like *I am a creation of God. God is abundant. I must be what I came from. Being like what I came from means that God wants me to enjoy the fullness of prosperity. This is how I'm going to express life from now on.* If necessary, print these affirmations and refer to them until they're a perfectly balanced reminder. Your lack is not God's fault. You have choice, so you choose to reconnect to abundance or stay out of balance, believing that that is God's plan for you.

2. There's a Limited Supply

This thought represents enormous resistance to a restoration of balance on the prosperity/scarcity scale. Thoughts such as *There's only so much to go around*, and *Everyone can't be wealthy; we need poor people to sustain a balance in the world, so I guess I'm just one of those poor people* are similar thoughts of limitation and won't attract a prosperous life. In fact, they'll make that aim absolutely unattainable.

Once again, the solution for removing this kind of resistance is to purge it, and replace these thoughts with new energies that match up more harmoniously with the truth of the world that you live in. Try thinking of money in the context of the ocean: There's an infinite supply, more than enough to take care of your needs. The supply of money circulating around this globe isn't diminished no matter how much you take for yourself. Why? Because ultimately, money, like ocean water, has to return to its source. It just keeps circulating as energy. Take a million gallons from the ocean, and it still remains the same.

Here's how it works—abundance is scooped from abundance, and abundance remains. You can purge the idea of shortages from your mind completely and begin seeing money as energy in infinite supply. It's necessary for life, just like air, water, nitrogen, and carbon.

3. I Don't Deserve it

Here's a simple rule of thumb: when you don't believe that you're worthy of prosperity flowing into your life, then you'll attract precisely what you *do* believe, which is, of course, a flow of scarcity and lack. If you believe that attracting money into your life is in some way inconsistent with a spiritual consciousness, then you erect barriers of resistance to stop this flow.

If you desire to live an abundant life and you're attracting the opposite, then obviously you're energetically out of balance. Your desire is highly spiritual, but what you offer that desire is your feeling of unworthiness. And the Universe being what it is, it submits back to you precisely what you believe about being undeserving. To change this idea and rebalance yourself on this scale, you need to realign your desire with the energy of your thinking.

You need to keep reminding yourself that

you are a Divine piece of God. Feeling as if you're unworthy of God's abundance is the same as denying your spiritual essence and insulting your Creator as well. Remember that you came here to be just like God, but you broke away from that idea when you believed more in your separation than in your unity with your Source.

Begin to change this out-of-balance attitude by cultivating an inner affirmation until it becomes second nature. Silently repeat something similar to: *I am a piece of God, a Divine, individualized expression of God. I am worthy and deserving of all that God is and all that flows into my life. The abundance I desire is on its way, and I will do everything I can to avoid blocking and resisting this Divinely inspired flow.*

4. I Have Limited Abilities and Talents

If you hold a belief in your mind that you don't possess the ability *or* talent to attract abundance, then you've weighted your balance scale with a lifetime supply of scarcity. This is a huge symptom of resistance, masquerading as an excuse for why you're coming up short on the prosperity balance beam. Reread the observation made by Ayn Rand. She didn't say, "It's the degree of talent that determines how far a person will rise." She said emphatically, "The degree to which he thinks" is the determining factor.

Your inner vision will trump your innate talent every time. In fact, if you have the confidence that the skills or abilities you need are readily available, then you're on your way. The first and most important step is releasing any excuse that you've adopted about lacking ability. Then it's crucial that you create an inner picture of yourself already living a prosperous life, even though it's failed to materialize yet. This is called *thinking from the end*. It forces you to begin an action programme that's in balance with your inner picture.

Now, and this is a crucial part, you must *become the abundance* that you desire. That's right—you must *be* it, rather than looking for it outside yourself. These three steps help you eliminate the idea that you're where you are because of a dearth of talent: (1) banish the excuse of no talent, (2) create an inner picture of attracting prosperity, and (3) act *as if* by *being* what you desire. You're as talented as you've *decided to be* up until now. Change the picture... and, miracle of miracles, you change your talents as well.

I was frequently told as a young boy, and even as a college student, that I didn't possess the necessary talent to be a writer or public speaker. It wasn't until I decided to follow my own inner pictures that my talents began to be heard. Why? Because the more I pursued my life from the balance point of what felt right for me, the more practice I gained, and the more the Universe and I were aligned. In that alignment I attracted and recognized all of the opportunities and guidance available to me. Had I listened to those who professed to know better concerning my talents, I would have attracted precisely what I was believing: an absence of ability.

5. I've Never Been Lucky

The Universe that you live in, and that lives in you, operates on energy and energy alone. "Nothing happens until something moves," said Albert Einstein. Everything is vibrating, even what seems to be motionless. Your Universe functions with the Law of Attraction, meaning that energy matches up with similar energy. Your thoughts are vibrations of energy. Low thoughts—those that are out of balance with Source Energy—attract low-energy responses from the Universe. High, spiritually based thoughts activate identical vibrations that bring you what you desire in harmony with your Source. That being said, there's no room for luck in the Universe.

If you have an accident, you aren't unlucky and you're not at fault. You're simply a vibrational match to whatever you collided with in that moment. By viewing your world in this way, you can begin to exercise more choice about what you're matching up with. By changing the lower vibrational energy of your thoughts to higher vibrations, you set into motion energy that seeks to match your higher desires. Even if this sounds nonsensical to your ego-trained mind, I urge you to begin the process of seeing things from a vibrational, rather than a good-luck versus bad-luck, position.

That is, I recommend that you adopt this belief system: that you've attracted into your life exactly what you've chosen to align with. If your luck appears to be bad, shift your expectations around. Make every effort to stay in balance with what you do desire, rather than what you've been attracting. Luck will disappear as a factor.

6. It's Always Been This Way

When you use your personal history to justify why you're presently out of balance on the abundance scale, you're really saying, *I have a long history of attracting scarcity into my life, and I intend to continue doing precisely the same thing.* Thinking that the past is responsible for your continuing insufficiency is a major source of resistance. You've probably been taught that if you don't pay attention to the mistakes of the past, you're bound to repeat them. Here's my take on that advice: *Keeping your thoughts on the mistakes of the past guarantees that you'll continue manifesting them in the present!*

I think you're better off tossing out your personal history of any deficiencies that have surfaced in your life. Refuse to think about what's failed to materialize unless you're hoping for more of the same. Avoid talking about your bleak past. Don't identify yourself as someone whose childhood or early adulthood was characterized by dearth and paucity. Instead, look upon your entire history as a series of steps you absolutely needed to take in order to bring you to the present realization of your endless potential for abundance.

Be grateful for all that failed to show up. Then shift from resistance to the direction of manifesting your desires, and rebalance your thinking so that it matches up with those desires. Affirm: *It is my intention to think thoughts that vibrate perfectly with my desire to be abundant in all areas of my life. I release any and all thoughts that put my focus, and therefore my pulling power, on what has or hasn't been.* This is the key to restoring balance.

7. I Don't Know How to "Think Abundance"
for Myself

When you're convinced that prosperity consciousness is akin to a foreign language, once again you've opted to *resist* rather than *allow*. You may not believe that you have the capacity to think in the ways that I've elaborated in this chapter, but I assure you that you do—in spades! You, the Rockefellers, the Hartfords and the Kennedys all emanated from the same Source of unlimited abundance. It is you, and you are it. Your belief that you can't think in these ways exists only because you've allowed yourself to believe in your separation from your Source. You can *think abundance*—even if you've never practised it your entire life.

Right now in this moment, you can initiate the practice of allowing only prosperous thoughts to live in your consciousness. Replace *I don't even know how to think like this* with *I am abundant, I attract prosperity, I am in balance with this desire, and I will not think in any other way*. That's how new habits are created. Make this your reality, one thought at a time.

To paraphrase Ernest Holmes, all of this adds up to expressing your life to fulfil God's law of abundance. Your existence is a gift from a thriving, plentiful Source of wellbeing. Being in balance means that you're expressing life by radiating this awareness with your thoughts. Consequently, your expectations support a beautifully balanced life in form.

This message from the great Sufi poet Rumi encourages you to begin each day with high vibrations of expectation that you're open to messages from your Source:

The breeze at dawn has secrets to tell you,
don't go back to sleep.

I remember this every morning as I awake (in what is actually the middle of the night for most people), and that morning breeze reveals secrets to me at the dawn of every new day. You're entitled to all of God's blessings. Being in balance is one of the secrets. Try it, and whatever you do, don't go back to sleep!

Chapter Seven

*Fighting Any Adverse
Condition Only Increases
Its Power Over You*

*(Balancing Your Desire to Live
in a Peaceful World
with Messages of
Evil Continually
Bombarding You)*

Chapter Seven

On a daily basis, we hear from a variety of sources that our world is turned upside down, evil exists everywhere, and terrorism is a way of life. People seem determined to kill each other in increasingly violent ways, while young children are recruited to become suicide bombers in the name of God. Radio, television and online news outlets dispense an endless cascade of man's inhumanity to man, family members gone berserk, teenagers on killing rampages in their schools, and terror cells rocking Earth's consciousness everywhere from train stations to places of worship.

I could go on describing the ways in which we're continually bombarded by the media, but I'm going to stop because I'd be violating the central premise of this chapter. The point I'm making here is that we *seem* to live in a totally out-of-balance world where our desires for feeling peaceful are challenged by the myriad nonpeaceful energies that are considered newsworthy. But we do have a choice in this matter. And we can choose to realign ourselves energetically with our desire to live in this world peacefully, regardless of what's going on around us, and in spite of the nonpeaceful energy we're so often subjected to.

We can begin by deciding to maintain a tranquil existence within ourselves even when others promote fear, anger, and hatred about this violent planet. After all, a massive collective effort throughout the history of humanity—by those in positions of authority—has taught individuals whom to fear, and even worse, whom to hate. If we'd been alive in America back in the 1750s, we'd have been told that it was our patriotic duty to hate the French as well as the Native Americans. Twenty-five years later, we'd have been told that it was okay to stop hating the French, but that we were obliged to hate the British. Now fast-forward 87 years, and if we lived in the South, we'd be told to hate those in the North, and Northerners likewise were required to hate Southerners, even if they were related by blood. (And by the way, it was no longer a requirement that we hate the British.)

Now move ahead 34 years, and it wasn't necessary to hate the Spanish, plus it was acceptable once again to love those who lived in a different latitude in our own country. Twenty years later, it was fine to love the Spanish, but compulsory to hate the Germans, and in just a few decades the Japanese would be added to our required hate list. Then it became all right to stop hating the Germans and Japanese, but we had to hate Communists, be they in North Korea or North Vietnam several years later.

In other words, there's always been a collection of people being added to or deleted from the hate inventory. For a long time we were required to hate Russians, then Iranians; we could love the Iraqis, but only for a short time. Then we reversed those on the hate list: we were obliged to hate the formerly loved Iraqis, and it was okay to love the Iranians that only ten years before we were told to hate. Then came the Taliban, and even more obscure categories such as terrorists whom we used to be required to love; and insurgents, whoever they are now, became mandatory targets of our hate.

On and on goes this litany of hate! The faces change, but the message remains: we're told whom to hate, never for a moment recognizing that the enemy we're supposed to hate isn't a nationality — *the enemy is hatred itself!*

Removing Yourself from All Hate Lists

Arthur Egendorf, writing in *Healing from the War*, offers this advice that's pertinent to our efforts to rebalance our life and to live peacefully:

Only together will we create a culture that supersedes the cycles of battle and retreat—not through our fear of war but through mastering a superior way to live.

The seed of this culture is the determination within individuals, and then small groups and communities, to devote our lives to the greatest vision of all time: not to wait for a savior one day to deliver us; not to wait for a government to pass truly just laws; not to wait for a revolution to right the wrongs of a cruel world; and not to mount a crusade to overpower some distant source of evil beyond ourselves. Each of us, singly and with all the others, is answerable for creating joy through the way our lives unfold, here and now. And once this purpose becomes primary, we can turn to the endless job of bringing wellbeing to others, justice and integrity to our government, and instituting constructive programs for change here and elsewhere. When inspired in this way, we don't have to wait for the final outcome before we're nourished. There is no finer way to live or die.

The words that speak loudest to me in this sagacious observation are: "Each of us, singly and with all the others, is answerable for creating joy through the way our lives unfold, here and now." I suggest that the number-one thing you can do singly to create joy is remove hate from your inner consciousness. This may be surprising, but please let it sink in. Those who hate war are just as responsible for the presence of war as those who hate their assigned enemies and fight to kill them. Those who hate crime are part of the crime problem. Those who hate cancer make cancer a foe and become part of the cancer problem.

Like everything else in this book, the secret to rebalancing life is not necessarily to change your behaviour as much is it is to realign yourself and *create a culture that supersedes the cycles of battle and retreat.* Whenever we use force to resolve our disputes, we instantly create a counterforce. This is largely responsible for the never-ending cycles of war that have defined human history. Force, counterforce, more force, and the battles go on, generation after generation. This is true within you as well: a thought of hate creates a thought of revenge, and then more hateful thoughts in response. And the real problem is that these thoughts of hatred and revenge begin to define your existence. They become your point of attraction.

Your initial desire to live peacefully, in a world that the media reports has gone berserk, is a spiritually balanced desire. In order to materialize your desire, you must extend thoughts that match the energy of that desire. Thoughts of hate will not blossom into your desired peacefulness, and the reason has been repeated throughout this book: *You attract more and more of that which you desire to eradicate.*

Breaking the Cycle

You can detach yourself from thoughts of hatred, despite the news from a media driven by a profit mentality. The more you buy into hatred, the more those who sell the messages benefit. But you can decide that you'll be an instrument of joy. So how does an instrument of joy react to a cacophony of loud, disturbing news? If you're in balance, you're most likely able to access the place of love and peace that you are. You remember your mission, and you desire to be in balance and peaceful by asserting that even though millions of others elect to be in hatred, this is simply not your calling. You didn't decide to incarnate into a world where everyone has the same vision. Your thoughts turn to: *I am a Divine creation; I choose to stay connected to this Divinity in all of my thoughts and in all of my actions.*

Then what do you do when you hear about people blown up by terrorists, or any other actions that are decidedly nonpeaceful? Here's what I remind myself to think and say: *I want to feel good (God). I didn't sign up for war or war-like thoughts. I'm an instrument of peace, and I send peaceful, loving thoughts to those people and places in the world who seem to need it so desperately. I refuse to collaborate with the energy of hatred anywhere, any time.* The alternative to this kind of peaceful thinking are anger, hatred, and fear, which align perfectly with the energy that is so distasteful—and your immediate reaction is to then seek revenge. A counterforce is established, and you're aligned with the same energy of hate that caused you to feel less than peaceful.

What if, in response to suicide bombers, we tended the injured and grieved the dead, but didn't publicize the tragedy with news reports? What if no one reported the consequences of this kind of violence? No news reports. No film. What if we chose to respect the pain of the relatives and survivors by not commercializing pictures of their grief? What if this kind of thinking surfaced when these acts of hatred took place?

The people who perpetrate these incidents are acting out of their own thoughts of hatred, hoping that others will respond in kind and that hatred will continue unabated. But if it was no longer news, if no one gave them attention, their acts would necessarily have to come to a halt. You, personally, can be one of those people who stubbornly refuse to add low-energy thoughts to the hate you observe. By doing so, you can contribute to the demise of hatred. You can act singly to create more joy by steadfastly refusing to be hateful in any of your thoughts. You break the cycle of violence in the world not by hating violence, but by being your own instrument of peace.

Choosing to Experience Peace by Focusing on What You Are For

The passage from the Holy Koran at the beginning of this chapter states that *whatever good you have is all from God* and *whatever evil, all is from yourself.* Having accessed your higher energy, you can process the out-of-balance events that humans create from a perspective of God-realization. There's no hate in God; there's only love. You can experience peace by balancing all that transpires around you with God-consciousness. There's nothing that requires you to react to evil-doing with a nonspiritual mental response. You have a choice to put your mental energy into what you desire, and in so doing, create a new world.

Let me tell you how I choose to respond to the bombardment of messages that focus on what's wrong in the world. First, I remind myself that for every act of evil there are a million acts of kindness. I choose to believe that people are essentially good and that by staying in this belief system, I help bring more of this consciousness to fruition. When enough of us take on this holy notion that whatever good we have is all from God, we'll learn to live collectively in this peaceful awareness.

Second, I know for certain that no amount of hatred in my heart will ever bring about peace. Hatred will only contribute more to the presence of those human-made destructive energies. So I choose to place my attention on what I am for, and on my feeling *good*, or feeling *God*. I support peace, not war. As Albert Einstein once remarked, "I am not only a pacificist but a militant pacifist... Nothing will end war unless the people themselves refuse to go to war." I, as a recipient of The Einstein Award from the Albert Einstein College of Medicine of Yeshiva University, would humbly add, "... and unless people refuse to ever think warlike thoughts".

In *Long Walk to Freedom*, Nelson Mandela wrote: "To make peace with an enemy one must work with that enemy, and that enemy becomes one's partner." I know that we are all partners with each other as children of God. This is how I think, and when I see footage of a world that's in disarray because many have forgotten this, I still choose to feel God's presence in me and know that we'll ultimately learn to live this way collectively. But it begins with each of us refusing to be instruments of nonpeace in all of our thoughts, and, consequently, all of our behaviours.

Adolf Hitler's designated successor, Hermann Goering, is quoted in *Nuremberg Diary* as saying:

Why, of course, the people don't want war... But, after all, it is the leaders of the country who determine the policy and it is always a simple matter to drag the people along, whether it is a democracy or a fascist dictatorship or a Parliament or a Communist dictatorship... voice or no

voice, the people can always be brought to
the bidding of the leaders. That is easy. All
you have to do is tell them they are being
attacked and denounce the pacifists for lack
of patriotism and exposing the country to
danger. It works the same way in any country.

I choose not to be one of
those people who are dragged
along. I refuse to be brought to the
bidding of any leader who attempts to
convince me that my beliefs in peace make me
unpatriotic. When an unidentified Pentagon
official was asked why the U.S. military censored
graphic footage from the Gulf War, he responded,
"If we let people see that kind of thing, there
would never again be any war."

Well, that is my goal... to live in a world where warlike thoughts are impossible because we're placing all of our mental energy on what we are for rather than what we hate. Former President Dwight Eisenhower, who was also a commander of the Allies in World War II, once remarked:

Every gun that is made, every warship launched, every rocket fired, signifies, in the final sense, a theft from those who hunger and are not fed, those who are cold and are not clothed. This world in arms is not spending money alone. It is spending the sweat of its laborers, the genius of its scientists, the hopes of its children. This is not a way of life at all in any true sense.

This is a call to get ourselves and our world in balance. Peace demands heroic thinking and a purity of conscience. When I remember this, I stay within my personal desire to live a God-realized life.

Third, when I see and hear evil, I remind myself, *I didn't sign up to come here to be a part of hatred. While others obviously have, I'll remember to stay with the inner sense of peace that calls to me, and I'll surround those who behave in evil ways with the same light energy.* I simply refuse to go to war in my thoughts. I choose to be a beacon of light for the places of darkness that are bereft of this kind of illuminating energy.

Finally, as the dispatches of violence continue

to come my way, I remind myself over and over again that we have a choice in how we respond to all of this. I know that by feeling hateful in response to hate, I only contribute to the presence of hatred in the world, and I also bring myself to a much less God-realized place. As an ancient Chinese proverb tells us: "If you decide to pursue revenge, you'd better dig two graves."

I know that we have the choice to put our energy into showing our love for God by loving each other. And I know that I have a choice to see what's good about the world rather than what has gone wrong. When those communiques of violence and hatred come streaming toward me, I push the mute button or even the off button, and I recall what the Dalai Lama once said:

Compassion and love are not mere luxuries.
As the source of both inner and outer peace,
they are fundamental to the continued
survival of our species.

Those are extremely valuable words describing our need to be in balance. I stay balanced on this dimension of being in a peaceful world by saying them over and over again. I now know for certain that I'm obliged to stay in a consciousness of compassion and love—not only to maintain my own balance, but to help ensure the continued survival of our species. There can be no greater calling.

.

Chapter Eight

Love Is What's Left Over When Falling In Love Fades Away

(Balancing Your Desire for Love with Feelings of Not Having Enough Love)

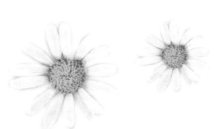

Chapter Eight

Love is something that we desire, and why not? The more love we receive, the more we feel loved and the better we feel. Feeling good (or God) is feeling balanced and in perfect harmony with our Source of being. Obviously then, one of our highest and most fervent wishes is to be the recipient of an endless flow of love. So what creates this huge imbalance between what we desire and how we feel? There's irony involved in the correction of this imbalance, and the observation of D. H. Lawrence in the opener spells it out perfectly.

As with all of the major imbalances I've written about in this book, rebalancing always involves an energy realignment that isn't achieved simply by memorizing strategies, or by adopting new behaviours. Rather, it's essential to know what kind of vibrational energy patterns you're sending to your desires. In this case, your desire is to feel good by having as much love in your life as you can balance. This can't be accomplished by demanding it, or by seeking it from outside yourself.

The key part of the quotation from Lawrence is "only the loving find love, and they never have to seek for it". Later in this chapter I'll return to these significant words. However, before looking at ways to implement this concept into your life, I want to explore Lawrence's assertion that "the loveless never find love". If there's too little love, does that mean, at least in Lawrence's interpretation, that we're *loveless*? Let's examine this notion.

The Loveless Factor in This Imbalance

If you're not receiving the love you desire, it seems like a pretty good idea to explore what's creating this state. Obviously, most of us want to place the blame for lovelessness on something external to ourselves. That's a waste of time and energy, but it often feels good because blame seems to alleviate the pain, even if only briefly. However, blame energy only helps you remain out of balance, whether you're blaming yourself or someone else. Being in balance is centered around the premise that you receive in life what you're aligned with. By now, you must have read it enough times to know that I mean that *you get what you think about!*

While you may justify your loveless state with thoughts of being unappreciated, or choose to see the whole world as an unloving place, the fact remains that you're experiencing the imbalance of not feeling good because you don't have enough love in your life. Waiting for others to change, or for some kind of shift to take place in the world to restore you to balance, won't work without your commitment to take responsibility for changing your way of thinking. If that's left to others, you'll turn the controls of your life over to someone or something outside you. And that's a prescription for disaster.

The point I want to emphasize here is that if feelings of being shortchanged in the love dimension are a part of your life, then it's because you've aligned your thoughts and behaviours with lovelessness. How do you do that? By failing to match your desire for love with thoughts that harmonize with this powerful desire—for example: *I've never been able to sustain a loving relationship. I'm not really attractive enough to have someone love me in the way I want to be loved. People are cruel and take advantage of me. I see hostility and anger everywhere. This is an uncaring world with a shortage of love.*

All of these thoughts (and others like them) create a point of attraction that's way out of balance with a desire to receive abundant love. You attract into your life precisely what you're thinking about, and you've inadvertently joined "Club Loveless" with a membership that includes a majority of the entire population—that is, people who feel shortchanged about the amount of love that's failing to pour into their empty hearts. All of this is reversible by shifting your alignment and removing the resistance to the fulfilment of your desire for love. You begin by ending your search for love.

No More Searching

So what does the poet mean by "those that go searching for love only make manifest their own lovelessness"? Well, when you seek something, you feel that what you're striving for is missing from your life. If it's love, for example, then what you're really saying is: *I'm experiencing lovelessness, and in my seeking I hope to fill this void.* But the problem with this approach is that rather than filling the love void, it only puts you further out of balance, and lovelessness continues to be your experience. Why? Because you're weighted more in lovelessness than in lovingness. Your thoughts are focused on finding what's missing, while your desire is for love to flow into your life.

This kind of misalignment continues to attract more of what's missing. What you're thinking about is the love that's not there. The Universe cooperates by matching up vibrationally with precisely what you're thinking about. How does the Universe know to do this? Well, it's merely matching its vibration to your thoughts through the Law of Attraction.

You need to turn off the searchlights and dismiss the search party, and instead replace them with an energy of loving thoughts—an internal knowing about receiving love. You originated from a place of Spirit that's defined by love. When you begin rebalancing your life so that your desire and the way you think and behave are a loving partnership, you'll realize that your desire is really God-realization.

The longing for love is a longing to become more like God in your thoughts. With this awareness, you soon realize that searching outside yourself for what you already are is the ultimate folly. No one else can give this to you— as D. H. Lawrence says, "the loveless never find love". This is because the loveless are focused on *not having* what they desire, rather than on what they already are.

Furthermore, the loveless believe that they're unworthy of the love they desire, and guess what? They continue to attract more evidence of their unworthiness. With the searchlights turned off, and the one-person search party given a permanent rest, you can turn your attention to balancing the authentic means at your disposal for receiving abundant love. This, then, is the irony, summed up perfectly in the poet's conclusion that "only the loving find love, and they never have to seek for it".

Becoming the Love

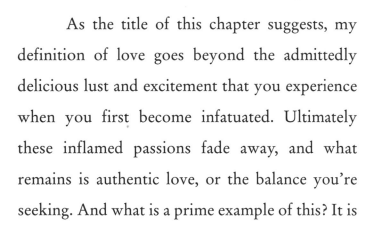

As the title of this chapter suggests, my definition of love goes beyond the admittedly delicious lust and excitement that you experience when you first become infatuated. Ultimately these inflamed passions fade away, and what remains is authentic love, or the balance you're seeking. And what is a prime example of this? It is to love as God does—to extend the caring that defines your very creation outward, whenever and wherever possible.

Love of this nature leads you to forget about your own ego, and want what you desire for yourself even more for another. This is how the act of creation seems to work. Your Creator doesn't ask anything from you in exchange for giving you life—it's given freely and abundantly, and no one is excluded. You don't have to repay God for giving you this life or the air you need in order to live or the water you drink for your very existence or the sun that sustains you. Without any of those freely given ingredients, you wouldn't continue to live. This is the love that God offers you.

To balance your life with more lovingness, you need to match your thoughts and behaviours with those of your Source, being love in the way that God is. This means noticing when you're inclined to judge yourself or others as though you or they are unworthy of love. This means suspending your need to be right in favour of being kind toward yourself and others, and deliberately extending kindness everywhere. This means giving love to yourself and others rather than demanding love. This means your loving gesture of kindness is heartfelt because you feel love flowing from within—not because you want something in return. A tall order? Not really, unless you believe that it's going to be difficult.

Lovingness is a feature of your natural

state, and your ego isn't part of that state. Ego dominates because you've separated yourself from your God-self, the loving self that came here from a place of perfectly Divine unconditional love. You've carried this ego idea of your own self-importance, your need to be right, for so long that you've deluded yourself into believing that the ego-self is who you are. Talk about being out of balance—you've opted for a belief in pure illusion! By allowing this illusion to be the dominant force, you've created, through your ego-centered self, a heavy imbalance in your life.

The result is that you want to feel love—the real thing, the love that is the very essence of your being, the love that you are—but you feel emptiness instead of lovingness. Why is this so?

Because the emptiness can only be filled with love by opening your heart connection to the spirit of love that originates you know not where, but can be felt within you. It's *your* empty space; no one else's. Therefore, only *you* can fill it. Your objective is to ask love within you to make its presence known, to have an awareness of being so full of love that this is what you have to give away. That's all you have to do—ask and receive. By doing just that, you'll attract more of what you're giving away.

You Can Only Give Away What You Have Inside

The restoration of this imbalance is dependent upon your willingness to reconnect to your Source of being and become an instrument of love. You must vow, from this moment forward, to see yourself exclusively in loving terms, and to invite love to accompany you 24/7. Here's an affirmation to help keep you on this path: *Holy Spirit, guide me now.* This simple, powerful statement aligns you with love. Self-contempt or self-rejection cannot distort your balance; you only have love to give away. When you give contempt or rejection to yourself or others, you're a vibrational match to these energies, and they'll continue to appear in your life.

Many people blame others (or an unloving, uncaring world) for the lack of love they're receiving in comparison to what they desire. Any disparity that exists between the love you desire and what you actually receive is a mirror image, a reflection of what you're thinking. Give away hate, and you receive hate; give away love, and it has to come streaming into your life.

Imagine a container the size of your heart. This container is the sole source of all thoughts. Whenever you think something, you must go to this container, select a thought, and send it out into the world. Using this metaphor, the real issue isn't about simply selecting positive, loving thoughts and having your world shift back into balance. The real issue is what's in the container—that is, what's in the heart reservoir you have inside you to give to others. This container within is connected to an endless supply of love; you need only turn your thoughts to that Source to be filled with love: love for yourself, love for the world, love for life, love for all others, and most significantly, love for your Source of being. Then this is all that you'll have available to give away, and consequently, all that returns to you.

It's been said that the difference between all of us living at ordinary levels of human consciousness and those we call saints is that they never forget God even for a single moment. They're cheerful when life is difficult, patient when others are impatient, and loving when others respond with hatred. Why? Because of that container. Ordinary people have a container out of which they pluck loving thoughts in certain circumstances. The saint has an internal vessel that contains nothing else, out of which and into which love flows freely.

So rather than working on simply changing your thoughts in order to become more peaceful and loving, why not shoot for the moon and think like the saint that you are? Focus on that container within. When you continually say, *Holy Spirit, guide me now*, you'll see your container over-flowing with so many loving thoughts that it's impossible for negativity in any form to alter the balance within.

What Love Looks Like Through the Eyes of a Child

Here are some jewels describing what love is, from the perspective of a group of four- to eight-year-olds. As you work to reset the "love balance beam" of your life, consider these refreshing thoughts on what love is.

- *When someone loves you, the way they say your name is different. You just know your name is safe in their mouth.*

- *Love is when you go out to eat and give somebody most of your French fries without making them give you any of theirs.*

- *Love is when my daddy makes coffee for my mommy, and he takes a sip before giving it to her to make sure the taste is okay.*

- *Love is when Mommy gives Daddy the best piece of chicken.*

- *During my piano recital, I was onstage and I was scared. I looked at all the people watching me and saw my daddy waving and smiling. He was the only one. I wasn't scared any more.*

And my favourite:

- *Love is what's in the room with you at*

Christmas if you stop opening presents and listen.

There you have it. Look within and around. Listen. Love is what's left over when falling in love fades away because love is an endless source. Give it away. Share your French fries. Give someone the best piece of chicken. Wave and smile to the Universe, and you'll soon know what Victor Hugo meant when he observed, "Love is the reduction of the Universe to a single being."

Not only is love what's left over when falling in love fades away, but love defines the Source from which we came. Elizabeth Barrett Browning poetically describes the end of life as a return to pure love:

> *Guess now who holds thee?—*
> *"Death," I said. But there*
> *The silver answer rang—*
> *"Not Death, but Love."*

And so it seems that love is truly all that's left over when this body falls away as well.

Chapter Nine

Earth's Crammed
with Heaven

(Balancing Your Spiritual Life
with Your Material Life)

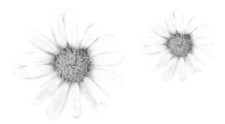

Chapter Nine

Heaven should not be thought of as a place you'll ultimately arrive at once you leave this earthly existence. Rather, it seems to me that you'd want to experience Heaven right here on Earth. As the title of this chapter suggests (from a poem by Elizabeth Barrett Browning), Earth itself is crammed with Heaven. But do you see Heaven in your daily life? Do you feel as if you're in a Heavenly world? If the answer is no, then you're out of balance. You've probably made your physical world the primary focus of your life, with little or no attention given to the Heavenly part of your earthly existence.

What This Imbalance Looks Like

When you place the larger part of your life energy on the material world, you are generally in a continual state of worry about your "stuff", and you feel like you never get ahead in the game of life. Virtually all of your mental energy is focused on what you have or don't have. You assess your worth based on such material issues as what kind of automobile you drive or how fashionably you're dressed. You may even feel inferior because other people have *more* stuff! This imbalance between the spiritual and material world usually means that indebtedness is a way of life. Your desire to have bigger, better, and more expensive stuff leads to borrowing money and greater financial obligations. Before long, debts exceed your ability to pay for those material acquisitions.

When you're overly involved with the physical, to the exclusion of the spiritual, you place a heavy emphasis on winning, becoming number one, and comparing yourself to others. A preoccupation with the material aspects of life leads to looking at life in a superficial way, where appearance is viewed as more important than substance. In fact, how it looks supersedes how it feels. What others think is the most important measuring device, and how you stack up to externally imposed standards, become all-important.

A devastating aspect of spiritual/material imbalance is the amount of time and mental energy

spent on monetary considerations. Money becomes the single most important standard for evaluating everything, including your happiness, inner peace, and feelings about your value as a human being. Everything is measured on a grid of monetary price or cost: *How much is it worth? How much does it cost? Can I afford it? Will it hold its value? Should I insure it? What if someone stole it? Could I afford to replace it?*

Your inner world is crammed with thoughts of costs and cash value. On your imaginary balance scale, the heaviest side is weighted down with thoughts that emerge from a consciousness where appearance, performance, and acquisitions are all that you notice. This consciousness prevents you from recognizing that right here, right now, wherever you reside is crammed with Heaven. Rather than looking for Heaven on Earth, you're condemned by your thinking process to live with the consequences of this disproportionate view of life.

The Impact of Imbalance

When you're out of balance, with life heavily weighted down on the material side of the scale, you pay a hefty price. The most serious consequence is that you see yourself in a false manner. Your true essence is spiritual, rather than physical, but you're unable to recognize this.

Your infinite self is never born and never dies. When you tip the balance scales in favour of the material world, you're identifying with an unstable ally that's forever changing. Your body, your possessions, your achievements and your finances are all ephemeral. They come and go like the wind. Every time you think that you've arrived, whether it be physical appearances or loads of money, something will change. In these arenas, you will always revert to some form of striving, uncertainty and anxiety.

Your preoccupation with being so materially weighted down on the balance scale is full of stress and worry. Your obsession with your body and how it looks turns into bitterness and angst as it goes through the aging process and leaves what you thought was the "real you" as only a memory, an illusion that can't be recaptured.

Similarly, your possessions wear out, become antiquated, lose their value, or just disappear. Because of your imbalance in this dimension, you're left feeling empty, purposeless and cheated. All of your hard work and dedication to your acquisitions, achievements and reputation become almost meaningless. The outcome is disappointment, regret, and perhaps even hostility toward the world. But this is not the world's fault—all of this anxiety that leads to stress is avoidable if you opt to balance the material/spiritual scale. Just a balance, an even split between these two aspects of yourself, is all you need to achieve.

The title of this chapter, "Earth's Crammed with Heaven", is meant to signify that it's all right here, right now—not in some other place, in a distant future years from now, or after the death of your physical self. Heaven is right here, now, at this time ... when you find your balance point.

Equalizing the Balance Scale

Heaven is a state of mind, not a location, since Spirit is everywhere and in everything. You can begin equalizing your material and spiritual life by making a conscious decision to look for the unfolding of Spirit in everything and everyone that you encounter. I personally do this by making an effort to look upon my world as if I were observing it through lenses that filter out the form and all of the material aspects of what I'm seeing, and I can only view the spiritual energy that allows what I'm noticing to exist. Try putting on these imaginary magical lenses and see how different everything appears. The natural world is a pleasant place to begin this experiment.

— **Nature**. When you look at a tree without these imaginary, form-filtering lenses, you may see branches, blossoms, leaves, and perhaps mangoes or plums. With your enchanting new lenses, the lines that form tree boundaries dissolve, and there's an energy vibrating so fast that it gives a whole new perspective of the tree. You see the spaces between the leaves and notice the silence of the now-defunct acorn or mango pit out of which the first sprout of creation emerged, jump-starting the whole process that eventually became the tree you're looking at.

You see the continuation of this life-giving process residing deep within the tree that lets it sleep in the winter and blossom in the spring, on into infinity (or at least for the duration of its life). You realize that new mangoes are producing not only new fruit, but an infinity of mango trees as well. You see this life force in just one tree, extending backward and forward in a never-ending stream of creation.

Begin looking at all of nature with this new vision—birds, ants, lakes, mountains, clouds, stars—all of it. Deepen your vision so that you no longer see only form and boundaries. Appreciate the miracle that is your environment... as you do so, you're getting into balance.

— **People.** These new lenses allow you to see everyone in a fresh perspective. You're no longer seeing tall and short, dark and light, male and female, old and young, beautiful and homely. Your lenses blur the lines that categorize people by cultural or religious differences, and you don't see others as only their attire or physical appearance or the language they speak. All appearances dissolve through filters in your lenses and your thoughts, so you now see the unfolding of the spiritual energy in every person you encounter.

What you notice is pure love vibrating

right before your eyes. You see kindness personified; you see and feel the same vulnerabilities in all others that you feel within yourself; you see enormous strands of peaceful, glimmering energy connecting each of us. Your new outlook invites you to playfully imagine that two people created you, and four people created the two people who created you, and eight people created the four people who created the two people who created you.

As we go back a few more generations to the time of Abraham Lincoln, there are 16,000 people you're related to who had to come together to create you! We can imagine going back to the time of Socrates, and puzzle over the apparent math we come up with. Trillions of people were needed to create one of us, but trillions of people haven't existed, so somehow, in some mathematically puzzling way, we're all related to each other. These are the kinds of fascinating connections that you can begin to observe with your imaginary lenses transforming your thoughts. You discover that there's no one to judge, no one to hate, and no one to harm, because you see clearly that we're related. In fact, we're all one. From here, you can extend your perspective to include more of life.

— **Events.** Where you once viewed the comings and goings of people as pure happenstance in current time, shaping the events of your life and the lives of everyone else, your new filtering lenses allow you to see how all of these things are connected energetically. Now you see an infinite network of laserlike energies emanating from the thoughts of everyone, blending the events in everyone's life in energetic perfection. You see some people with very fast vibrations of energy matching up perfectly with the energy of the Source of creation. You see how they attune with the all-creating, all-knowing Source of life, and how events are perfectly attracted in a vibrational match.

You also see what appear to be accidents, tragedies, and horrors, and how they, too, are vibrational matches that collide in what you've called "mistakes", but are really the result of two or more energies meeting in a larger picture that you couldn't previously see. You witness the connection between the expectations of individuals and what they attract into their lives. With these amazing lenses, you note that all events and all "accidental" encounters are really incredibly compatible vibrational matches, rather than randomly occurring situations. With this awareness, you're attaining a level of balance between Spirit and form.

How Life Looks When You Have a Balance Between Spirit and Form

Here's what I've found as a result of being able to keep these twin aspects of life in balance. I now see spiritual energy in everyone I encounter. When I'm tempted to judge anyone, I remind myself to view them through my special lenses. When I can do so, all negative judgment dissolves. I feel more peaceful knowing that I'm not just this body that I'm destined to discard. I also feel the life-giving Spirit within me on a daily basis, and it's exhilarating! I now know that I'm an infinite spiritual being and that I share this originating energy with everyone on this planet, as well as everyone who's ever lived here or will live here in the future.

Being more balanced spiritually and physically gives me the opportunity to be in a continual state of gratitude and awe. I see miracles everywhere. I take myself less seriously. I feel intimately connected to others. I have less stress in my life. I feel less pressured to fit in, or to accomplish more. And the irony is that I perform at a higher level because Spirit flows unimpeded through me.

There's a significant change in your life when you correct the imbalance between your physical and spiritual being. The title of this chapter is taken from a well-known poem by Elizabeth Barrett Browning. Here is a portion of the poem:

Earth's crammed with heaven,
And every common bush afire with God;
But only he who sees, takes off his shoes,
The rest sit round it and pluck blackberries ...

When Moses approached a burning bush, he took off his shoes and communed with God. You can shift your focus and see with new eyes encouraged by your thoughts. When you do, you'll see that the poet is right: *Earth's crammed with heaven*. If you don't believe it and practise it, then you'll hopefully enjoy sitting around plucking blackberries.

Sogyal Rinpoche observed that "two people have been living in you all of your life. One is the ego, garrulous, demanding, hysterical, calculating; the other is the hidden spiritual being, whose still voice of wisdom you have only rarely heard or attended to…" I'm inviting you to restore some balance by looking for Heaven everywhere and listening and attending to that hidden spiritual being that is within you at all times, begging to you to pay it more heed.

About the Author

Dr. Wayne W. Dyer is an internationally renowned author and speaker in the field of self-development. He has created numerous best-selling books, audios and videos; and has appeared on thousands of television and radio programs, including *The Today Show*, *The Tonight Show* and *Oprah*.

Hay House Titles
of Related Interest

Books

Ask & It Is Given,
by Esther and Jerry Hicks

(The Teachings of Abraham)
Attitude Is Everything for Success,
by Keith D. Harrell

Confidence,
by Barbara De Angelis, Ph.D.

Eliminating Stress, Finding Inner Peace
(a book-with-CD),
by Brian L. Weiss, M.D.

The Gift of Peace,
by Ben Stein

I Can Do It®,
by Louise L. Hay

The New Golden Rules,
by Dharma Singh Khalsa, M.D.

Simple Things,
by Jim Brickman, with Cindy Pearlman

All of the above are available at your local
book shop, or may be ordered by visiting:
Hay House UK: **www.hayhouse.co.uk**
Hay House USA: **www.hayhouse.com®**
Hay House Australia: **www.hayhouse.com.au**
Hay House South Africa: **orders@psdprom.co.za**
Hay House India: **www.hayhouseindia.co.in**

We hope you enjoyed this Hay House book.
If you would like to receive a free catalogue featuring additional
Hay House books and products, or if you would like information
about the Hay Foundation, please contact:

Hay House UK Ltd

292B Kensal Rd • London W10 5BE
Tel: (44) 20 8962 1230; Fax: (44) 20 8962 1239
www.hayhouse.co.uk

***

Published and distributed in the United States of America by:
Hay House, Inc. • PO Box 5100 • Carlsbad, CA 92018-5100
Tel: (1) 760 431 7695 or (800) 654 5126;
Fax: (1) 760 431 6948 or (800) 650 5115
www.hayhouse.com

Published and distributed in Australia by:
Hay House Australia Ltd • 18/36 Ralph St • Alexandria NSW 2015
Tel: (61) 2 9669 4299 • Fax: (61) 2 9669 4144
www.hayhouse.com.au

Published and distributed in the Republic of South Africa by:
Hay House SA (Pty) Ltd • PO Box 990 • Witkoppen 2068
Tel/Fax: (27) 11 706 6612 • orders@psdprom.co.za

Distributed in Canada by:
Raincoast • 9050 Shaughnessy St • Vancouver, BC V6P 6E5
Tel: (1) 604 323 7100 • Fax: (1) 604 323 2600

***

Sign up via the Hay House UK website to receive the Hay House
online newsletter and stay informed about what's going on with
your favourite authors. You'll receive bimonthly announcements
about discounts and offers, special events, product highlights,
free excerpts, giveaways, and more!
www.hayhouse.co.uk